Rising Star

A view of the winery in front of the Domaine Chandon offices.

Rising Star

DOMAINE CHANDON: A DECADE OF SPARKLE

Text by

Jamie Laughridge

Illustrations by

Veronica di Rosa

Published and distributed by Hopkinson & Blake, New York

Copyright © 1983 by Hopkinson & Blake, Publishers

Published by Hopkinson & Blake, Publishers
1001 Avenue of the Americas, New York, NY 10018

Manufactured in the United States of America

Library of Congress Cataloging in Publication Data

Laughridge, Jamie.
   Rising star.

   1. Domaine Chandon (Firm).   2. Sparkling Wine—California.
   I. Title.
TP557.L38   1983   338.7'663224'0979419   83-8569
ISBN 0-911974-31-8

"Come quickly! I am drinking stars!"—Dom Pérignon

Edmond Maudière, consulting enologist for Domaine Chandon, with a life-size wax likeness of Dom Pérignon.

Photo by Malcolm Hébert

Acknowledgments

Many thanks to these people, who generously shared their time, expertise, and memories with me.

The entire Domaine Chandon family
Maxwell Arnold
    Maxwell Arnold, Jackson & Smyth
Tony Baldini, Trefethen Vineyards
Robert Lawrence Balzer
Jim Beard
    Napa Valley Wine Library Association
David Berkeley, Corti Brothers
Arlene and Michael Bernstein
Margrit Biever, Robert Mondavi Winery
Frédéric Chandon, Moët-Hennessy
Alain Chevalier, Moët-Hennessy
Randy Chinn, D & M Wine and Liquor Co.
Jack Davies, Schramsberg Vineyards Co.
John A. De Luca, Wine Institute
Ghislain de Vogüé, Moët-Hennessy
Joe Elmiger, Westin St. Francis
Bill Essertier, Young's Market Co.
Ed Everett, The Wine Trade
Phillip J. Faight, Cakebread Cellars
Al Falchi, The Waterfront
Tom Ferrell, Franciscan Vineyards
Jerry Gabriel
    Environmental Planning and Research
Tony Giovanzana, Coit Liquors
Jack Goldenberg, Old Peoria Company
Louis R. Gomberg, The Gomberg Report
Robert Gourdin, Schieffelin & Co.
Webb Hansen, Young's Market Co.
Stu Harrison, Wilson-Daniels
Jack Hennessy, Jack P. Hennessy Co., Inc.
Claire and Philip Hiaring
    Wines & Vines
Gerald A. Hirsch
    Heritage Wine Cellars, Ltd.
Dorothy Hopkins, Burson-Marsteller
David Kay, 9-0-5 Stores, Inc.
J. Penn Kavanagh, Schieffelin & Co.

Peter Korzilius
Tony A. LaBarba
    American Wine & Importing Co.
J. Michael Lynch, Pacific Wine Co.
Edmond Maudière, Moët & Chandon
Herb McGrew, Pickle Canyon Vineyards
André Mailhan, Café Argenteuil
Louis P. Martini
    Louis M. Martini Winery
John Overall, The London Wine Bar
Bernard Portet
    Clos du Val Wine Co., Ltd.
Frank Prial, The New York Times
Belle Rhodes, Bella Oaks Vineyards
René di Rosa, Winery Lake Vineyards
Angelo, Bob, and Buck Sangiacomo
William J. Schieffelin, III
    Schieffelin & Co.
Don Schmitt, The French Laundry
Peter M. F. Sichel
    H. Sichel Söhne, Inc.
Barry Stein, Goodmeasure
Margaret Stern, Seagram Wine Co.
Janet and John Trefethen
    Trefethen Vineyards
Claude Uson, Café Argenteuil
Renate Wright

And special appreciation to
Anne Luther, Judy Ostrow,
Linda McGrew, Michaela Rodeno,
and John Wright.

—Jamie Laughridge

for Robert-Jean de Vogüé

Frédéric Chandon (left), Alain Chevalier (foreground),
John Wright, and Edmond Maudière (with wine bottle).

Foreword

Since its foundation nearly two hundred and fifty years ago, Moët & Chandon, the most successful champagne house of all, has always been receptive to new ideas.

This willingness to innovate – as long as, and only if, quality can be maintained – is reflected in the character of its Californian daughter, Domaine Chandon.

I paid my first visit to Domaine Chandon's vineyards in 1975. The winery was still in the hands of the builders and I had to wear a steel helmet while being shown round, but I was able to sample the early cuvées. Composed under the expert guidance of Moët's enologist, Edmond Maudière, they displayed promise of great things to come.

Now, ten years after Domaine Chandon's founding, none would dispute that the wines produced in the architecturally arresting, ultra-modern winery have fulfilled, exceeded even, that promise.

What I find so inspiring about this achievement is that, although the parent firm has given lavishly of its wine-making expertise and its investment resources in this first decade, it has left Domaine Chandon free to grow and flourish with a style and business flair that are wholly American. No mere transplant of the French parent to American soil, Domaine Chandon embodies the spirit and enthusiasm that has marked the rapid growth of the Californian wine region to world stature.

Europeans, with their many centuries of history, might never be so bold as to reflect on a past spanning only a decade. In publishing this book, Domaine Chandon has asserted its American birthright: a right to be unbound by, though respectful of, tradition; to break new ground; and to act with the speed that has marked so many great American business success stories.

PATRICK FORBES

Patrick Forbes is the author of "Champagne: The Wine, The Land and The People", published by Victor Gollancz Ltd., London. Now in its fifth edition, his book is often referred to, even by the French, as "The Bible of Champagne".

Contents

Château de Saran.

*I*t was 1968 — a year when American eyes focused on the sky. Three men orbiting the moon — Borman, Anders, and Lovell — drew our gaze upward, and reminded us that ideas were not earthbound. In France, Count Robert Jean de Vogüé, then chairman of the board of Moët-Hennessy, was also thinking of expanded horizons. Under his direction, Champagne Moët & Chandon had already begun production of sparkling wines in Germany and Argentina. It was an inspired move, considering that peak production had been reached in the delimited Champagne region and that bad harvests could create shortages in the marketplace. Was North America the next logical location for Moët-Hennessy to explore? An upcoming trip would help its chairman decide. Soon, de Vogüé would eye California's Napa Valley — much as Americans eyed the stars — and have the courage to say, "Why not?"

THE COUNT IN CALIFORNIA

The trip that convinced de Vogüé to make California his next target was a one-and-a-half month jaunt through the United States, designed primarily to introduce the count's son, Ghislain, to Moët-Hennessy customers. One of the last events on their itinerary was a San Francisco sales meeting in honor of the de Vogüés' visit, sponsored by Moët-Hennessy's San Francisco distributor, Juillard Alpha.

CHAPTER ONE

Star on the Horizon

13

The meeting was to begin at 9:00 a.m., but the count, a man with a reputation for punctuality, did not arrive on schedule. "When he was not there by 9:45, I became anxious and went to check his room," says the younger de Vogüé. "My mother assured me he had left well before nine." Now quite worried, Ghislain went in search of his father. He finally found him in a meeting room off the main corridor, sitting near a small stage with a group of strangers.

"Father, you're in the wrong meeting," he said, before noticing the bottles of California wine in the room. "No, I'm not," said the count, who was delighted to have stumbled into a meeting of California winemakers. "What I'm doing here is far more important. Tell them to start without me," he said.

As Ghislain de Vogüé pulled his father down the hall, the count spoke animatedly of the future. "I definitely want to start an operation in California," his son remembers him saying. "Their wines are superb and they are very congenial people." Though the chairman would not rush into this American venture, his decision was made. Moët-Hennessy would some day produce sparkling wines in California.

A REVOLUTIONARY IDEA

Today, the thought of a Frenchman wanting to make wines in California is easy to imagine.

In 1968, the idea was considered revolutionary, both in France and America. The United States had always been a minor market for traditionally-produced French champagne, and U.S. demand for California sparkling wines made by the costly *méthode champenoise* was even smaller. According to estimates, fewer than 150,000 cases of domestic méthode champenoise sparkling wine were produced annually in the late sixties—hardly a burgeoning market. The risks of entering this segment of the sparkling wine business in California were compounded by the costs and labor-intensive nature of the time-honored method.

It made sense that Count Robert-Jean de Vogüé would favor the revolutionary idea of making méthode champenoise sparkling wines in California—he had always been something of a revolutionary himself. A war hero in the First World War, de Vogüé married into the Moët family and joined Moët & Chandon as managing director in 1930. During World War II he became a leader of the Resistance in the Champagne district, rallying everyone from the smallest *vigneron* to the major champagne houses to resist German occupation. After his arrest by the Gestapo in 1943, the count was condemned to death and deported to Germany. He was saved when British paratroopers liberated his labor camp in May, 1945.

In peacetime France, de Vogüé became known as "the Red Count," a champion of the workers, and helped Moët & Chandon earn its reputation as one of France's most progressive employers. Working with a local representative of the trade union, a man who had been one of his comrades in the Resistance, de Vogüé pioneered worker participation in 1947 that finally became French law in 1959.

The count was also revolutionary in his approach to marketing champagne. He believed that over the years the great champagne houses had lost sight of the importance of salesmanship. Houses that had sent representatives all over the world in the late 18th and 19th centuries to develop markets for champagne had a different attitude in the 20th. Proud of their full cellars, they waited complacently for orders from customers, as a debutante might wait to have her dance card filled. The count felt differently. *"Moi, je suis marchand de vin,"* he was known to say, happy to think of himself as a wine merchant. He realized that in the future the only opportunity for the growth of Moët & Chandon lay in exporting the expertise to make fine sparkling wine. "My father thought the champenois people should realize that the aura and glamor of champagne would lead others to imitate it. He thought if the French exported their know-how instead of their bottles, they could control the production of sparkling wines all over the world."

In the years following his chance encounter with the California vintners, Count de Vogüé thought a lot about exporting expertise, particularly to the west coast of the United States. With co-chairman Maurice Hennessy, he had helped build Moët-Hennessy – a conglomerate producing luxury products such as Moët & Chandon champagne, Hennessy cognac, and Dior perfumes – into an international company earning billions of francs annually. After his retirement in 1972, the 76-year-old count assumed the honorary chairmanship of the Moët-Hennessy board of directors. The advice he passed on to his successors was this: Champagne stocks are dangerously low, worldwide demand is growing rapidly. Export expertise, not just bottles. And when you look for new production opportunities, don't forget California.

THE CONSULTANT CUM GRAPEGROWER

In Brussels, meanwhile, another man with his eye on California was pursuing a path that would eventually cross with de Vogüé's. This was John Wright, who in 1969 was a senior consultant with the international management consulting firm Arthur D. Little, Inc. (ADL). Wright, a 1954 chemistry graduate from Wesleyan University, was a wine buff, a man

15

fascinated with the whole process of making and marketing wine. During an earlier assignment in ADL's New York office, he surprised his suburban Connecticut neighborhood by planting a small vineyard of French hybrids in his backyard. In Brussels he broadened his expertise by buying Burgundy in barrel from a wine merchant and bottling it in his basement on weekends. Eager to grow good wine grapes and make his own wine, Wright requested a transfer to ADL's San Francisco office in 1969. It was no coincidence that the Napa Valley was less than an hour from his new home.

Wright immediately began searching for vineyard land with his partner Herb McGrew, a New York friend from college days who had also been attracted to the wine country. One day in 1970, Wright picked up two hitchhikers who lived in the Mayacamas Mountains, the western border of the Napa Valley. They told him about a widow who wanted to sell some hillside acreage on Mt. Veeder. Wright and McGrew bought the property that summer, cleared it in the fall, and planted it with Zinfandel and Merlot in the spring of 1971, using labor from the nearby commune known as Jollity Farm. The partners named their new venture Pickle Canyon Vineyard.

Planting Pickle Canyon clinched it. Wright still was engaged in writing feasibility studies for ADL clients, but his heart was in grapegrowing and winemaking. This interest, combined with indications of a budding U.S. wine market, led him to propose a marketing study to ADL on the future of wine in America. The company liked the concept, and sold it to eight European companies for $20,000 each. Moët-Hennessy was not among them.

The study was completed in March, 1972. Called "Wine/America," it was a comprehensive report with enough facts, forecasts, and financial analyses to fill three thick volumes. Working with Louis R. Gomberg, a San Francisco consultant to the California wine industry, Wright made projections about future wine consumption in the United States. Americans, he believed, would significantly increase their consumption of table wines in the years to come, with premium table wines growing as much as 15% annually. More risky to predict was growth in quality sparkling wines, a relatively static market at the time. The rapid growth in sparkling wines during the sixties was largely due to sales of a sweet, fizzy wine called "cold duck," and nothing in the available consumer research indicated that this might change. "Wine/America," however, hypothesized that growth in premium table wine consumption would create a base of consumers who would understand that good sparkling wines are first and foremost good *wines*. "We thought growth in premium sparkling wines would lag the leading indicator, the table wine business," explains Wright.

MEETING MOËT-HENNESSY

A few months after completing "Wine/America," Wright got a call from ADL's Paris office. They were gathering information on possible investments in the United States for the Banque Nationale de Paris. Could Wright prepare a brief summary of his study for several potential investors? Wright did, and was invited to meet with some of those investors in Paris in July, 1972. Among them was Guy de la Serre, secretary-general of Moët-Hennessy. The meeting was pleasant, ending with de la Serre asking Wright if he would see two Moët-Hennessy principals during their trip to California later in the year. With ADL's approval, Wright agreed.

The following month, Wright resigned from his full-time position at ADL. His plans were simple: consult a little, enjoy his vineyard a lot. He was doing just that when Alain Chevalier, director-general of Moët-Hennessy, and Bertrand Mure, president of Moët & Chandon, arrived in California. ADL in Paris had arranged for Wright to meet the Frenchmen in San Francisco to discuss the general direction of the wine business in America. The next day, Chevalier and Mure visited Wright in the Napa Valley.

Today, John Wright realizes the significance of that visit. He mentions a leisurely walk on the golf course with the elegant, soft-spoken Chevalier, a man he had met only 24 hours earlier. "Chevalier said he really wanted a Moët-Hennessy presence in California, but that to acquire an established winery was not, in his opinion, a financially interesting proposition. His preference, he confessed, would be to start an operation from scratch, but the problem then became to find someone qualified and willing to manage it."

Wright was surprised at Chevalier's concern. "That's the easiest part!" he said. "There must be a hundred people in the area who would give their eyeteeth for such an opportunity." John Wright hadn't yet realized that Chevalier was sounding him out; might the part-time Mt. Veeder grapegrower be eager for the challenge?

The next move came quickly. Late in 1972, when Wright was in Brussels finishing an ADL project, he was invited to a meeting with representatives from ADL's Paris office, the Banque Nationale de Paris, and Moët-Hennessy. Chevalier was there, along with a distinguished man with an accent that sounded more English than French. John Wright didn't catch his name. He learned later the man was Kilian Hennessy, chairman of the board of Moët-Hennessy. By the end of the meeting, Hennessy and Chevalier had suggested that Wright

17

visit Epernay, home of Champagne Moët & Chandon. They weren't sending the Californian off to sip champagne; they were sending him to meet Moët-Hennessy's honorary chairman of the board, Robert-Jean de Vogüé.

The next week, Wright made the 65-mile trip from Paris to Epernay. It was October, and the hillsides of Champagne were at their most alluring. Wright stayed at the Château de Saran, a converted hunting lodge used to entertain special guests of Moët & Chandon. Looking out the window of his suite at the neat vineyards surrounding the chateau, he began to think seriously about Chevalier's interest in making sparkling wine in California. At the same time, he was having second thoughts about his own career as part-time consultant, part-time Mt. Veeder grapegrower.

THE CONNECTION IS MADE

When Wright and de Vogüé finally met on that October day in 1972, the rapport was instantaneous. After 45 minutes of spirited conversation, the count offered his plan. "John, I believe people are what really count in any business proposition. I've wanted an operation in California for some time and I think you're the right person to run it. I want you to be chairman of the board of our new company in America." While Wright was letting that statement sink in, the count was already giving him

his first assignment – see Renaud Poirier, *chef de caves* of Moët & Chandon. Poirier, the count explained, would go to California to set up a tasting of California wines. "I put all my confidence in Poirier," said de Vogüé.

Renaud Poirier, like his father before him, had once been chef de caves at Pommery, another leading champagne house. When he left Pommery in the late sixties, de Vogüé immediately invited him to join Moët & Chandon. In a milieu where most champagne makers knew much about the art and little about the science of winemaking, Poirier was a technical genius. His nose and palate were legendary.

The first meeting with Poirier took place in Moët's lab, amid the beakers and instruments that are part of the enologist's trade. *Oui,* said Poirier, he would come to America to taste wines. *Oui,* he knew precisely what should be included in the tasting. *Non,* he did not want finished sparkling wines included in the tasting – what would be the purpose? He wanted only to taste the raw material, the still wines that are the basis of sparkling wines. Wright struggled to keep up with the conversation in his less-than-perfect French. He recalls the shock of receiving, on his return to California, a letter from Poirier in impeccable English. Yes, the Frenchman wrote, he would be coming in December and he was most eager to evaluate the wines. Wright began to realize that the new venture might remain a dream if Poirier and his nose were not satisfied.

THE POIRIER TASTINGS

December 1972 was the start of a busy period for Wright. First, he installed Poirier at Silverado Country Club, "upwind of the nearby cattle feed lots so as not to disturb his nose." Then he searched out the varietal wines Moët's chef de caves wished to taste. Only wines from the current 1972 vintage interested Poirier. He wanted the laboratory analyses of the wines, and he wanted to know the nature of the microclimate where the grapes were grown. Although Chardonnay and Pinot Noir are traditionally used to make champagne in France, Poirier also wanted to taste a range of other grape varieties in California. One thing he had learned developing the Moët operation in Argentina was that you can't play by the same rules in every country.

The "Poirier tastings" were a turning point. After they took place, the venture was a definite go. Moët's chef de caves identified hillside vineyards as promising sources of good grapes for the base wines, although he was less enthusiastic about Carneros, a cool region south of Napa. He also asserted that he found Napa technically superior to the Sonoma and Monterey areas for sparkling wine grapes. This delighted John Wright, who was also con-

vinced that Napa Valley was the place to be, in part because of its well-earned prestige in the marketplace.

As 1972 ended, Americans were thinking about President Nixon's defeat of Senator George McGovern, or the war in Vietnam, or perhaps the economy. But when Auld Lang Syne played that year, John Wright had other things on his mind. He was planning the birth of a new star in the world of sparkling wine, a star to which he hoped to hitch his own.

19

20

Mt. Veeder.

By the start of 1973, Moët-Hennessy was ready to make it official: Napa Valley in California would be the site of its next venture in the production of sparkling wine, and John Wright would be the man to run it. Over the next few years, the parent company would provide millions of dollars in capital, the advice and expertise of its key people, and, inevitably, its own French cachet. Moët-Hennessy looked to Wright for his marketing sense, his problem-solving abilities, and the kind of contagious enthusiasm needed to spark any new venture.

CHAPTER TWO

Introducing M&H

The incorporation papers were signed on March 26, 1973, in San Francisco. Some details remained to be worked out, among them the name of the new venture. When the lawyer asked for the corporate name, director-general Alain Chevalier suggested M & H Vineyards, to represent the company's ties with Moët-Hennessy. Although Wright thought the nod to heritage appropriate, he admits he found the name undistinguished. "M & H" was, he joked, better suited for trading stamps or plumbing supply houses. But it was to appear only on the incorporation documents, not on a bottle of sparkling wine. There would be time later to select a more evocative name.

The lawyer also asked for the location of the new firm's corporate headquarters. Wright realized that the makeshift office in his garage on Mt. Veeder had no street address. Given a choice of any odd number between 1700 and 1900 (his relative position on Mt. Veeder Road), Wright chose 1743 – the year in which Moët & Chandon had been founded by Claude Moët.

BUYING LAND

The Mt. Veeder property was M & H Vineyards' first land acquisition. Some was covered with gnarled Zinfandel and Alicante vines, but much of the 200-acre ranch had been replanted as pear and prune orchards during Prohibition. As Wright knew from his own experience with the adjoining Pickle Canyon vineyards, Mt. Veeder was not the easiest place to start a vineyard. Much of the land needed clearing and parts were hilly enough to make tractor work dangerous. But as he and Poirier agreed, the property had good points to balance its drawbacks. The hilly topography ensured excellent drainage, a plus for keeping vine roots healthy. More importantly, the area had the cool climate that tends to produce good grapes for sparkling wine – grapes with low sugar and high acidity.

Cool climate was precisely what led M & H to its next land acquisition, in the Los Carneros region. In 1973 this area was still dominated by sheep ranches and hay farms. Located at the southern edge of the Mayacamas Mountains near San Pablo Bay, Carneros lies in a foggy area that benefits from the bay's afternoon breezes. This keeps it several degrees cooler than areas to the north; too cool, many thought at the time, to produce good grapes. It had long been assumed that the clay hardpan and shallow soil made any agricultural pursuit in Carneros a challenge. Except for independent grapegrower René di Rosa, Buena Vista Winery, and Louis Martini, few in the early seventies believed the area had real potential for producing grapes of quality.

The M & H group disagreed. By now, Poirier was semi-retired, and Moët's new *chef de caves*, Edmond Maudière, had replaced him as primary advisor to the new company. On an inspection tour of the Carneros ranch, Maudière and Wright decided its agricultural potential and price made it a good investment. Moët-Hennessy approved, and the land was purchased. This original Carneros acquisition covered 550 acres. (Later, 600 more were acquired.) Within the precisely delimited Champagne region, Moët & Chandon's vineyards total no more than 900 acres – one of the largest holdings in Champagne, an area where a single acre makes its owner a wealthy person.

M & H chose to buy land rather than an established vineyard for a simple reason: no one in the company could predict which grape varieties would be selected to produce the company's sparkling wine. Like Poirier before him, Maudière tasted the Napa Valley's varietal wines, sometimes as many as 20 or 30 a day. He had his theories about which would be best suited to sparkling wine production, and had even come up with some experimental blends—called *cuvées*—from six table wines he bought at retail. Chardonnay and Pinot Noir, classic components of champagne, would probably be among those selected, but in what proportions? Would they marry and age as they do in Champagne? Might not other varietals add desirable qualities to the blend? Experimentation would provide some answers; educated guesses would have to supply the rest.

BUILDING A STAFF

As M & H was acquiring land in the spring of 1973, it was also attracting a small staff. In a valley the size of Napa, no effort is needed to spread interesting news. With almost uncanny timing, people stumbled onto M & H, and found jobs waiting. Few fit the traditional mold of the agricultural worker. In fact, few fit *any* mold.

Among the early employees were Will Nord and Michaela Rodeno, both vice presidents with Domaine Chandon today. Rodeno had tracked down John Wright in his cinder block garage on Mt. Veeder after reading about the venture in a local newspaper story. She was hired to assist John, and her fluent French (the result of studies at the University of California, Davis and the University of Bordeaux) became invaluable in communicating with the parent company.

Will Nord was recruited to join the group by the late John Carmer, then vineyard manager on Mt. Veeder. Carmer felt he needed more technical expertise in getting the nursery started, and thought that Nord, his viticulture teacher at Napa Community College, could provide it. As a former consultant, Wright recognized the value of professional advice. Although he had learned a great deal about hillside vineyards while planting Pickle Canyon, he knew he needed outside expertise to develop commercial vineyards.

Nord remembers "wriggling his way up those crazy roads to Mt. Veeder" and talking to Wright about the new venture. In his typically impulsive way, Wright decided immediately that Nord was the man for the job and asked him to join the group. Nord agreed to become a consultant. It would be more than a year before he joined the company on a full-time basis, and in the meantime, he says, "I shook my head more than once at the social experiment."

The social experiment Nord speaks of was the inexperienced M & H vineyard crew—a group of workers who knew more about Woodstock than rootstock. Broadly speaking, they were of a counterculture bent, with an idealistic view of life. Few had any agricultural background and most were over-educated for their positions. Excitement at being part of a bold new venture was probably their best qualification. Working on Mt. Veeder and later in Carneros, they began to learn about sparkling wine, literally from the ground up.

WORK BEGINS

Ever since phylloxera—a root louse that attacks and destroys certain unprotected vines—swept through the world's wine-producing regions in the late 1800's, it has been necessary to graft vinifera vines (the traditional European wine varieties like Cabernet Sauvignon, Chardonnay, and Pinot Noir) onto resistant American rootstock to ensure healthy vineyards. At the start, Wright had decided M & H should build a nursery and graft its own vines rather than buy plants from a commercial nursery. "The motley crew," as the workers were often called, was given the task.

Maudière and Nord were part-time consultants, so the task of instructing the crew was often left to Wright. Being an enthusiastic amateur vineyard owner was one thing; supervising the American subsidiary of the famed house of Moët & Chandon was another. Wright lived just a few steps away from the garage-office on Mt. Veeder. Many a night he would go home tired and dusty, take down his copy of Professor Winkler's treatise on viticulture, and study what had to be done the next day.

By most accounts, that start-up period on Mt. Veeder was freewheeling, festive, and more than a little exhilarating—at least on good days. Workers generally began grafting, planting, pruning, or cultivating about 8:30 a.m., often alongside their overall-clad chief executive. If the managerial style was informal, the drink of choice was more high society. President and crew—generally decked out in an assortment of denims, faded work shirts, gauzy Indian-print shifts, and headbands—were frequently seen toasting the mastery of a new viticultural technique with Moët & Chandon Brut Impérial.

The occasional visitors to M & H in those early days provided a welcome opportunity to talk about the venture, take a break, and, sometimes, to celebrate. According to Wright, the first outsider to find M & H Vineyards' Mt. Veeder headquarters was a Jehovah's Witness selling The Watchtower; the second was wine writer Robert Lawrence Balzer. Dapper in his bow-tie and suit, Balzer knocked on the always-open M & H office door one day, taking Wright by surprise. How did he know where to look? Simple, Balzer replied. He had recently been to France, where his friend Robert-Jean de Vogüé suggested he drop in on Moët's new American subsidiary.

Regular visits were paid by various representatives of Moët-Hennessy, some of them titled gentlemen whose soigné appearance contrasted sharply with the attire of the laid-back California crew. The French, in their finely-cut suits and dressy leather shoes, would arrive at the unexpectedly primitive headquarters of the young company, eager to see the progress.

Despite their aristocratic manner, the visiting Frenchmen always took time to shake hands and talk with the crew. One of the early workers remembers that "it wasn't like you'd call them by their first name and slap them on the back, but they were friendly—not aloof."

Once when a high-level delegation from Moët-Hennessy arrived on a tight schedule, Wright decided the best way to quickly shuttle them around the valley was by helicopter. Some of the original vineyard crew still remember the excitement caused by the copter's arrival on Mt. Veeder. When the door opened, out came John Wright, chef de caves Edmond Maudière, director-general Alain Chevalier, and Count Frédéric Chandon de Briailles, vice chairman of Moët-Hennessy. The helicopter pilot soon found himself taking vineyard crew members for short flights over the mountains while Wright and the French team scouted the premises. It is difficult to say which group had the better time.

A few months earlier in 1973, Count de Vogüé had paid a visit to California to play some golf and see how his pet project was coming along. He was pleased to see the activity on

25

Mt. Veeder and amused that the workers were, as he told Wright, "not just heepies, but *retired* heepies." Not traditional agricultural types perhaps, but the count could see they shared his love of vineyards, and he found their enthusiasm charming.

One distinct memory Wright has of that visit was the day that the count, surrounded by the scruffily-dressed crew, christened the new nursery with a magnum of Moët champagne. To an outsider, it might have looked like a clash of cultures; to those present, it seemed marvelously appropriate.

FINDING A HOME

Also in the spring of '73, John Wright got a call from the real estate agent who had handled the Carneros sale. There was a piece of property for sale bordering the city of Yountville, in the center of the Napa Valley. Would M & H be interested? When Wright saw the property and heard the price, he knew his answer was "yes." Here were 350 undeveloped acres, ideally situated for the winery that M & H was to build. The land was near Highway 29, just where it narrowed to two-lanes; easy access to the winery would be assured for visitors. It was adjacent to a railroad siding. And although it was then a badly over-grazed cattle pasture, the natural beauty of the site was unaffected. This was the kind of setting where a jewel of a winery would really sparkle, and Wright knew it.

Maudière and Nord agreed with Wright's assessment after clambering over rocks and through patches of poison oak, looking at the site. Five or six acres on the edge of the parcel were planted in old Green Hungarian and Burger vines, and it looked as if 25 more acres might be planted. The decision was unanimous: this property would be an appropriate setting for the M & H winery. Wright bought it soon after, at $1,100 per acre. The poison oak and cattle would soon be banished. In their place four years later would stand the showplace headquarters of the first French-owned sparkling wine venture in the United States.

MEETING THE NEIGHBORS

Historically, outside investors were viewed with some suspicion, and often with more than a little hostility, by those who lived and worked in the Napa Valley. However, reaction to the news that the French were coming was generally positive, since Moët's arrival denoted a confidence in the future of Napa Valley wines that had never before been demonstrated by a prestigious European wine concern. But the hectic pace of the work in progress had not allowed time for getting acquainted with neighboring vintners and grapegrowers. In May 1973, Wright decided to have a party to introduce the new venture and its French backers to the Napa Valley.

The reception was a gala occasion and attended by many of the top vintners in Napa. Moët flowed and waiters proffered *hors d'oeuvres*. Guest of honor Robert-Jean de Vogüé—warm, cordial, and charming as only a Frenchman from Champagne can be—made it clear that Moët had chosen the Napa Valley because he thought it ideal for producing top-quality sparkling wines. The guests were understandably pleased.

The reception was the kind of gracious gesture typical of Moët-Hennessy and its Napa Valley offshoot, and it was appreciated by the close-knit circle of wine producers in the valley. Quite by serendipity, moreover, it put the fledgling company in touch with a family that would play an important part in its future—the Trefethens.

Gene Trefethen, president of Kaiser Industries, and his wife, Catherine, had owned a vineyard in Napa Valley since 1968. Mrs. Trefethen attended the M & H reception with her sister and brother-in-law, also Napa Valley grapegrowers. After a pleasant chat with Count de Vogüé and John Wright, she invited them to lunch the next day.

Wright recalls lunch at the Trefethens as a pleasant social occasion. A few days later, he and Nord were discussing wineries that might

be willing to make experimental lots of wine for M & H in 1973. Harvest was only three short months away. Few wineries had excess capacity, and even fewer were equipped for sparkling wine production. Nord suggested talking to the Trefethens. He knew their vineyard manager, Tony Baldini; perhaps something could be arranged. It's a possibility, thought Wright, remembering the recent lunch at Villa Trefethen—and the empty, 100-year-old building he had toured while there. With characteristic speed, he hopped into his car and headed down Mt. Veeder toward Trefethen Vineyards.

27

28

The Trefethen winery.

CHAPTER THREE

A Little Help from Our Friends

*I*n June of 1973, John Wright met John Trefethen, who manages Trefethen Vineyards for his parents. Things happened so quickly once they got together that looking back, neither quite believes the schedule. They met, they made plans, they outfitted an empty winery. Within two months, they were harvesting and pressing grapes.

The cooperative venture progressed smoothly because M & H and Trefethen Vineyards met certain of each other's needs. M & H needed grapes and a bonded winery to press and ferment them. Trefethen had the grapes and the building and had applied for a license to make wine commercially. Still, the Trefethens needed equipment and expertise to get their own winemaking efforts underway. A deal was struck whereby M & H offered to equip Trefethen's winery building in exchange for its use until M & H's own winery in Yountville could be completed. As in all good deals, both parties were getting what they wanted.

Now the race was on to get equipment in place before grapes were ready to harvest. Admittedly, the task that lay ahead was ambitious. The Trefethen winery, an historic three-story redwood structure built in 1886, was beautiful but barren. "No tanks, no press, no nothing," Wright remembers. Prior to the agreement with M & H, the Trefethens had ordered some equipment for their first small winemaking effort, but they planned to make only a small amount of wine. M & H – with its interest in experimenting with varieties and, with luck, getting a start on the sparkling wine operation – wanted to make much more. The Champagne consultants had ideas of their own about equipment.

As John Trefethen recalls, the first order of business was to get the building itself in shape. "We put a floor in the winery – it had been dirt – and repaired the roof." Getting equipment was more complex. Trefethen had planned on three tanks for their operation; M & H wanted at least 12. Unfortunately, stainless steel tanks aren't sold cash and carry. They would have to be manufactured to order. Would they get to the winery before the rapidly ripening grapes?

There was also the matter of a press. The Trefethens were planning to use only a small stemmer/crusher for this, their first crush on a commercial scale. Maudière wanted a press that would handle the grapes gently. Solution? Maudière arranged for a Vaslin press, the type used by Moët & Chandon in Epernay, to be air-freighted from France. "We were impressed," says John Trefethen's wife and business partner, Janet. Tony Baldini, vineyard manager for Trefethen, has other memories. "When we unpacked the press, we realized it was marked in metrics," he says, shaking his head. "And of course it wasn't set up for our electricity." But in short order, Baldini and the M & H crew had made the necessary modifications – rewinding the motors, finding adaptors for the fittings, recalibrating the gauges.

Summer flew by, blurring together visits from the French, searches for the right kinds of hoses and pumps, and frantic phone calls to the manufacturers of the stainless steel fermentation tanks and to the Bureau of Alcohol, Tobacco, and Firearms about the pending license. Some people in the valley wondered why M & H was in such a hurry. After all, the company had only been incorporated since March; might it not be better to take things slowly, to wait for the 1974 harvest to make those experimental lots? Was it really worth the struggle to make wine this year?

In the minds of Wright, Maudière, and the management of Moët-Hennessy, it certainly was. If the wines turned out to be good, they could be held in reserve for the first cuvées, putting M & H a year closer to producing a finished sparkling wine. If the wines from the first, experimental harvest were unacceptable for use in sparkling wine, they could be sold in bulk to still wine producers. Either way, M & H would have its first opportunity to see how California grapes reacted to winemaking methods traditional in the Champagne region but unknown in the Napa Valley. Experimental lots could be fermented and tasted, and the

30

young company would be closer to knowing what to plant on its vineyard properties.

MEANWHILE ON MT. VEEDER

Before Wright encountered the Trefethens, he had talked with Michael and Arlene Bernstein of Mt. Veeder Winery about using their new winery's facilities to make experimental lots of wine for M & H.

The connection between Wright and the Bernsteins was a friendly one. They were vineyard neighbors on Mt. Veeder, and the Bernsteins' partner in the winery, Kim Giles, was also working for M & H. Living in such proximity, they often shared information and ideas about vineyard development. In fact, Michael Bernstein remembers when Wright first suggested that French investors might be interested in making wine in California. "I told him I thought that was the craziest idea I'd heard in my life," he says. "Lo and behold, a few months later Moët-Hennessy announces it's coming to the valley and John tells me they've asked him to be in charge."

The Bernsteins, grapegrowers on Mt. Veeder since 1963, had built their small winery in 1973. They were happy about the prospect of its being used by M & H, in part because they expected to learn about winemaking from the French advisors involved in the project. Indeed, Maudière gave them precise instructions

about how the grapes should be handled. "He wanted us to use an Amos crusher from Germany and he had it air-freighted to our winery. As I recall, it cost about $3,200 to do that," says Bernstein.

Before the first grapes were ready to be picked, someone started thinking about the newsworthiness of this event. Wasn't this, after all, the first time Napa Valley grapes would be harvested for French investors, investors who also represented the biggest champagne house and

31

a wine tradition going back over 200 years? Wasn't this a story that might interest the media? Someone got in touch with a television station in San Francisco, which agreed to cover it.

The first grapes – Sémillon, from a vineyard in Pope Valley – arrived at Mt. Veeder Winery on August 18, 1973. All the equipment was unfamiliar, the building was small, and no one but Maudière was quite sure how to proceed. The Bernsteins didn't know where a camera crew could be squeezed in. It was disappointing but probably fortunate, then, when the station called to say they would not be coming. One of the major news stories of the year, the probe into Vice President Spiro T. Agnew's illegal activities, was developing. Franco-American grapes had been pre-empted by political scandal.

Although no camera crew was there to record it, the Sémillon was crushed successfully – the first of some 14 experimental lots. The Bernsteins crushed Chardonnay and French Colombard, as well as the last grapes from some ancient Zinfandel vines on the old Simmons ranch, now M & H's Mt. Veeder property. Blended with a little Petite Sirah, the Zinfandel was bottled as "Last Harvest Simmons Ranch" and shared by those who had picked the grapes and made the wine. Soon, the old vineyard would be ripped out and planted with new varieties. It remained for M & H to decide what those varieties would be.

THE CRUSH AT TREFETHEN

Almost miraculously, Trefethen was also ready to receive grapes by the end of August. A few fermenters were in place inside the winery, but the majority of the tanks were yet to arrive. On August 26, 1973, the first day of crush, tension was high. "The grapes were being picked, but we were still waiting for the inspector from The Bureau of Alcohol, Tobacco, and Firearms to give us final approval on our license," John Trefethen says. The bureau finally gave the word, and the crush proceeded as planned.

The grapes were picked at a relatively low ripeness by California standards, according to practice in Champagne. The intent was to reduce fruitiness in the wines and to maintain a high level of acidity, both factors that contribute to the desired delicacy of champagne. But the California sun makes Napa grapes ripen beyond the point where grapes in the Champagne region have reached their zenith. Picking at precisely the right moment is critical. As the harvest wore on, the sugar content of the unpicked grapes rose steadily. The few tanks already installed were quickly filled, but the grapes would not wait.

As more and more Trefethen grapes were delivered to the winery, prayers for tank deliveries became fervent. But since tanks often came while grapes were being pressed, installing them called for a bit of maneuvering. The press sat in front of the door, the only door large enough for the tanks to enter the winery. While some workers pushed the press out of the way, others rolled in the new tank. A winery worker was often a busy passenger inside the moving tank, cleaning it or installing fittings so it could be hooked up quickly to receive juice from the press.

JUDGING THE RESULTS

Several nerve-racking weeks later, M & H had completed its first harvest. Aside from some Green Hungarian and Burger grapes from the Yountville property, the company had bought all the grapes from local growers, including the Trefethens. They purchased 35 tons of Pinot Noir, 50 tons of Chardonnay ("Too much," Maudière says, laughing), 8 tons of Pinot Blanc, and 69 tons of assorted varieties such as Ugni Blanc, Sémillon, Folle Blanche, and French Colombard. It was Maudière's plan to taste and evaluate the new wines when he returned later in the fall. First, he had to return for France for Moët's harvest, a month later than in California because of the chill northerly climate of Champagne.

The tasting of M & H's experimental lots took place as planned in November, 1973. Bertrand Mure, Renaud Poirier, and Edmond Maudière came from France to taste the young wines. Some were rejected out of hand. (Comments from Poirier such as *abominable* and *inutilisable* need no translation.) The Chardonnays were a surprise. Each of the lots from four different vineyard locations was found to have excessive fruit and sometimes also the quality called *gout du terroir*—too much pronounced Chardonnay character for the intended use in sparkling wine. Perhaps, Maudière thought, the Chardonnay might be balanced with Pinot Blanc, which Poirier found to be *assez bon*.

If one lot stood out it was the Trefethen Pinot Noir, judged *bon* by the tasters. It was not, however, without problems. The new wine was *taché* (stained), giving it a tinge of color from the dark Pinot Noir skins that was considered undesirable for a classic-style sparkling wine. Maudière made a mental note: He would have to press these California Pinot Noirs very carefully to avoid too much color; in Champagne, the cold climate automatically kept "staining" from occurring in all but the greatest vintages.

When the tasting ended, Wright and Maudière knew their rush to crush had paid off. They now knew some varieties they liked, as well as some they didn't. No final decision was made, but at least they knew which varietals were still in the running. Better yet, they had their first reserve wines – Pinot Noir and Pinot Blanc – to hold for use when blending the first commercial cuvées. Both men felt that day was not far away.

DISCOVERIES AND INNOVATIONS

Already, M & H was bringing new ideas to the valley. The trend had been for growers and wineries to consider only efficiency when picking grapes and to use the largest containers available – often two, five, or even 10-ton gondolas to transport the fruit to the winery. In smaller containers there is less weight and therefore less pressure on the fruit. This means the grapes are more likely to arrive intact at the winery, which reduces damaging oxidation of the juice. "M & H specified that they didn't want big bins," says Trefethen's Baldini. "We fought it at first, since we were already set up for the usual gondolas, but then we started using smaller bins or picking boxes at their direction."

M & H's style of pressing – slow and gentle, with the grapes left in whole clusters – might have been new to the Napa Valley, but Maudière knew its advantages from his years of champagne-making. Because of the tendency of the Napa Valley Pinot Noirs to yield unwanted color, gentle pressing was even more important. Normally, newly-harvested grapes are dumped into a hopper, sent through a screw conveyor, then destemmed and crushed, and pumped into a press. M & H dumped its grapes directly from the harvesting bins into the press, eliminating excess handling. The rough stemming and crushing steps were skipped altogether.

One of the early experiments at Trefethen helped show the value of mechanical harvesting. Trefethen Vineyards had been planted to accommodate mechanical harvesters, but both M & H and Trefethen worried that grapes harvested by machine might not give results as good as grapes harvested by hand. A block of Chardonnay vines – the same age and pruned the same way – was chosen to test the theory. During the 1973 harvest, alternate rows were picked by hand and by machine. The grapes were kept separate throughout the processing and fermentation. Then a blind tasting was held to determine which lot was better. Not one taster could tell the difference.

This was good news. It meant that M & H's growers – and, eventually, their own vineyard managers – could pick at the precise moment the grapes reached the desired ripeness. Instead of frantically trying to put together a crew of laborers (often a time-consuming process), they could harvest the grapes as soon as the decision was made to pick. What's more, they could harvest 24 hours a day (crews were often reluctant to work around the clock.)

There was still the problem of color in the Pinot Noir grapes. Maudière had a theory about how to control it, and he decided to test it during the 1973 crush. The experiment took place at Trefethen, in the small lab adjacent to the winery. Maudière gave instructions that as each load of Pinot Noir was brought in from the vineyard a sample of the juice should be kept in a separate container and the time of harvest noted. When he examined the samples, they confirmed that color extraction intensified in the heat of the day, diminished in the cooler evening, and remained stable through the night. The course of action was clear—harvest the Pinot Noir grapes at night to keep the skins from leaching color into the juice. This would become standard operating procedure for those M & H growers whose Pinot Noir vineyards were trellised for mechanical harvesting.

By the time the harvest of 1974 rolled around, the staff of M & H had done an incredible amount of research, thinking, and brainstorming. Wright and other key people in the growing M & H family had logged several trips to France, Maudière had spent months in the Napa Valley, and other experts from Moët—including Philippe Coulon and Guy Gimonnet, enological and technical advisors—had visited California to analyze and report on technical aspects of the new venture.

Techniques used on an experimental basis in 1973—mechanical harvesting, night harvesting of the Pinot Noir grapes, and gentle pressing—became standard techniques in 1974.

By the end of the crush, M & H knew much more about the sparkling wine business. It had crushed 310 tons of Pinot Noir (almost five times as much as 1973), nearly 53 tons of Chardonnay, and, significantly, 21 tons of Pinot Blanc and about 28 tons of Ugni Blanc (grapes Maudière hoped could balance the fruity Napa Valley Chardonnays). The miscellaneous

35

varietals crushed – such as French Colombard and Chenin Blanc – had slackened off to a mere 4 tons, compared with the 69 tons of the first, experimental harvest.

In November, 1974 it was again time to taste the new wines and to decide which might be used in a first commercial cuvée. The final decision rested with Edmond Maudière, a man with the pedigree for the job. A fourth-generation champagne maker, Maudière had blended his first champagne cuvée at age five, making the base wines on a tiny press he had built himself. As chef de caves of Champagne Moët & Chandon, his nose and palate were the guiding force behind Moët and its "super-cuvée," Dom Pérignon. He had also consulted on Moët-Hennessy's winemaking efforts in Germany and South America. He knew that blending the first California cuvées would be a challenge; who could predict precisely how the base wines would marry and mature? Past experience in Champagne could guide him, but it certainly could not supply him with a detailed map.

For that very reason, blending the first cuvées (a process known as *assemblage*) was particularly exciting. Assisted by M & H winemaker Sergio Traverso, Maudière tasted, made notes, and tasted again. The key, he knew, was to assemble a perfectly balanced blend; "smooth like a ball, with no pits, no holes, no disparities." It must be pure, because bubbles would magnify its taste, good or bad. To create this balanced beginning, he would use the new wines from 1974, plus the reserve wines from 1973. Together, they would enable him to create the blend he had in mind as a model.

He soon found the balance he wanted, basically two parts Pinot Noir to one part Chardonnay, with some Ugni Blanc to soften the Chardonnay. Like a chess master, Maudière was constantly thinking several moves ahead as he tasted and blended the wines. He knew the cuvée would evolve and mature in the process of becoming sparkling wine and that he must anticipate how the delicate blend would react at each stage. The sparkling wine born of this cuvée would not be available to the public until December, 1976, to allow sufficient time for aging. By then its separate components – perhaps four different varieties from 26 different vineyards – would be seamlessly married.

While he was blending the first cuvée, Maudière had an inspired thought, totally contrary to practice in Champagne and potentially risky in the United States market. The lots of Pinot Noir he was tasting were exceptional, if colored unacceptably. Might it not make sense to blend a special cuvée, comprising only these excellent Pinot Noir wines? He thought back to

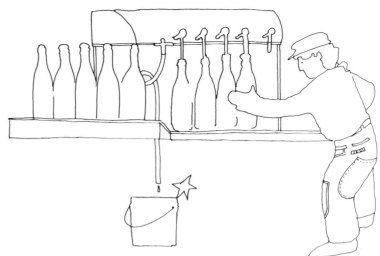

the distinctive nose of his grandfather's *blanc de noirs* champagne, which he could still vividly recall. Yes, M & H could have its own blanc de noirs cuvée, an almost-white sparkling wine made from black grapes. It would have a lovely, full-bodied taste, and just a pale blush of the color sometimes compared by the French to the eye of the partridge, *oeil de perdrix*.

John Wright loved the idea of the 100% Pinot Noir cuvée. Some in France remained to be convinced of its marketability because of the deservedly poor reputation of the pink sparkling wines known as rosé champagne in the U.S. During a private tasting at Moët of M & H's cuvée from the 1974 harvest, one question came up repeatedly. "Edmond, you're not really going to bottle the Pinot Noir, are you?" The answer was yes – 40,000 bottles.

FIRST TIRAGE

The first M & H cuvées were bottled in the spring of 1975 on the upper floor of Trefethen winery. Preparations for the *tirage* (from the French *tirer*, to draw, because the cuvée is "drawn out" from the tank to the bottle) began soon after the 1974 harvest. Champagne bottles were located and purchased, machines were ordered, bottling techniques were argued over and finally settled on. Such knowledgeable Napa Valley neighbors as Jack Davies

of Schramsberg Vineyards willingly shared the benefit of their experience. Nonetheless, the first tirage was trying. It was also a lot of fun.

Imagine the scene: Ten enthusiastic novices, president Wright among them, trying their best to master the bottling process, a process that permits only a small margin of error. If the amount of sugar added to the bone-dry assemblage is too small, the sparkling wine will not have enough effervescence; too much, and the bottle will explode under the pressure caused by excessive carbon dioxide from the fermentation.

Mechanically, tirage is not just a process of filling bottles and sealing them, as the M & H crew soon learned. After the bottle is filled, a small plastic plug (called a *bidule* – French, literally, for "whatchamacallit") must be inserted into its neck. Only then can the metal crown cap go on, providing the tight seal needed to contain the mounting pressure of the carbon dioxide from the secondary fermentation in the sealed bottle.

37

The challenge, then, was to fill, "bidule," and crown-cap 150,000 bottles in a matter of weeks—using the most primitive machines. After a slow start and many sore muscles, that's exactly what the crew managed to do. It was hardly an efficient production line. As one worker remembers, "Any time one thing went wrong, the whole line screeched to a halt."

When John Wright wasn't working on the bottling line or calculating the number of champagne yeast cells in a rapidly multiplying culture, he could be found in Trefethen's large dumpster, packing down waste cardboard cartons in which the bottles had arrived from the manufacturer. That's where he was the day the representative from the State of California Alcoholic Control Board arrived, asking for someone who could tell him about the new M & H operation. "Why, I can," Wright volunteered from his post in the dumpster, "I'm John Wright." Disdainfully, the man asked what he did around here. "I'm the president," answered John, brushing off his coveralls and extending his hand.

TWO WINERIES, ONE ROOF

From the first crush in 1973 until 1977, M & H maintained some part of its operation at Trefethen Vineyards—tantamount, John Wright says, to the confusion of two families sharing one bathroom. And, indeed, a bathroom was to play a part. Maudière, among other things a microbiologist who had studied at the Institut Pasteur, brought his own strains of champagne yeast from France to aid in the fermentation of the wine, since these yeasts are known for their ability to ferment under adverse conditions such as low temperature, high alcohol, and increasing pressure. Important to their healthy development was finding a room where the ambient temperature could be stringently controlled. Maudière decided that one of the Trefethen winery bathrooms was as close to an ideal spot as he would find, so he moved in his precious yeasts and closed the room to its usual function. Even visiting dignitaries were politely informed it was off-limits.

Until M & H's Yountville winery was ready to store bottles of aging sparkling wine, the ground floor of the historic Trefethen winery was bonded as Trefethen Vineyards; the second floor was under a separate bond and license as M & H Vineyards. This was primarily because federal regulations regard the transition from still wine to sparkling wine as a major event, one worth considerably higher tax revenues (and, therefore, higher bonds). Every time wine moved from one level to another, a transfer form had to be filled out. "The paperwork was overwhelming," Janet Trefethen recalls.

Another challenge came in dealing with the difference in the two firms' production. Trefethen made still wines; M & H made sparkling wines. This distinction became very important to the government when it discovered that Trefethen Vineyards was storing sugar in its winery. In California, this is illegal for those who produce still wines, but perfectly legitimate for those, like M & H, who use it to cause a secondary fermentation in their sparkling wines.

Sometimes, the problems of shared space became startlingly evident. John Trefethen recalls walking into the winery one day to see a pipe near the ceiling bent downward a good two inches. About to complain about the bad installation, he took a closer look. "I realized the ceiling had sunk under the weight of those 150,000 bottles, each weighing nearly four pounds," he says. "I saw very dramatically how much heavier champagne bottles are than regular wine bottles." Within a few days, the second floor of Trefethen Vineyards was shored up, and an engineer was called to check its tolerance. "He gave us an answer we didn't want to hear. Needless to say, we called in another engineer."

Those first 150,000 bottles undergoing secondary fermentation caused more than their share of worry. They were arranged *sur lattes*—in neat stacks lying on their sides—in massed blocks about four feet high. Chunks of cork blocked the end bottles in each row. At the time, the Trefethen's Labrador puppy, Ethel, was going through her chewing period. "We'd be hard at work when Ethel would come bounding up, proudly bearing a piece of cork," says Janet Trefethen. "Then someone would have to run upstairs and madly search to find where it had come from."

Anyone who remembers M & H back then speaks of the sound of exploding bottles. During the hot summer, many a bottle of soon-to-be sparkling wine exploded as the heat increased the pressure of the gas trapped inside. The sound was startling, and often, so was the after-effect. Since the second-story wood floor of the winery wasn't watertight, those below got a cooling shower of sparkling wine whenever a bottle blew.

From the moment the first bottles of sparkling wine were stacked in Trefethen's old wooden winery, John Wright had nightmares of earthquakes. But mostly he dreamed of the new winery taking shape up the road.

40

Dapples, hauling rocks for the construction of the winery.

CHAPTER FOUR

Yountville Takes Shape

M & H had purchased its winery property, originally a parcel of 350 acres, in 1973. It was a beautiful piece of land in the heart of the Napa Valley—a rolling expanse in the Mayacamas foothills, just west of the tiny town of Yountville.

Before the arrival of M & H, Yountville was chiefly known as the site of the State of California Veterans' Home, the residents of which accounted for half the town's population of 2,800. The town was named for George C. Yount, the first American to settle in Napa Valley. The story goes that when Yount first stood on Mount St. Helena in 1831 and viewed the area that would later bear his name, he doffed his coonskin cap and was inspired to say, "In such a place I should love to clear the land and make my home. In such a place I should love to live and die." That phrasing might have been a bit dramatic for John Wright, but standing on a high hill, surveying the M & H property, he could certainly understand Yount's sentiment.

As word spread that the French-owned concern planned to make its headquarters near this small town, the response was often a surprised, "Why Yountville?" The place was not—like St. Helena to the north—a picturesque tourist attraction; besides, it was located south of most of the Napa Valley wineries that drew visitors to the area. Perhaps the town made up in potential what it lacked in charisma. As former mayor Don Schmitt puts it, "Yountville was a little town just waiting for something to happen to it."

One of several things that happened to Yountville in 1973 was getting M & H Vineyards for a neighbor. The fact that the property lay just outside Yountville brought on some discussion among the town fathers about annexation. In spite of the potential for broadening Yountville's tax base, the idea was eventually killed. Many people, Mayor Schmitt among them, felt this decision was a wise one because the town simply wasn't equipped, financially or administratively, to provide the services a sizable business might expect. Better, they decided, to leave the property under the county's jurisdiction, subject to the agricultural district zoning rules.

GETTING UNDERWAY

The cooperative winemaking venture with Trefethen relieved the immediate pressure for M & H to build its winery. Still, Wright wanted to construct suitable headquarters as soon as possible, and step one was to find the right architect. This was easier than anyone might have anticipated. One day, when his son, Gerald, was entertaining a friend on Mt. Veeder, Wright casually mentioned the plan to build a winery near Yountville. Gerald's guest announced that his father was an architect and would surely be interested in the project.

Not long after, Wright met with the young man's father, Bob Mountjoy, a partner in the San Francisco-based firm of Rockrise Odermatt Mountjoy Associates (ROMA). At the first meeting, Wright learned that ROMA was well-known for its planning work in park areas such as Yosemite and the Grand Canyon. ROMA's sensitivity to the environment appealed to Wright; he wanted special attention paid to the physical surroundings of the proposed winery. "We talked with a few other firms, but I was immediately impressed with ROMA's approach to design problems," he says. "From the start, I felt we could work together."

First impressions were right. ROMA and M & H were well-matched. By the end of 1973, several preliminary meetings had been held and siting work was underway. As part of the process, Bob Mountjoy and his family spent a weekend camping on the site to observe the wildlife, the play of natural light, and generally to absorb the spirit of the area. The field trip paid off. ROMA's initial site recommendations meshed with Wright's personal vision of the winery, and the architects were given the word to proceed.

FORM FOLLOWS FUNCTION

"They started, as all good architects do, from the inside out," Wright recalls. In this case, the key to the inside was understanding the business of producing sparkling wine. Project architect Jerry Gabriel was familiar with the intricacies of still wine production, having worked on the design of both the Robert Mondavi and Freemark Abbey wineries. Although not specific to sparkling wine production, this knowledge gave ROMA a general foundation. From there, the design team developed more specialized expertise through regular meetings with Wright and Maudière.

The challenges of the M & H winery project were clear from the outset. Both Wright and Moët-Hennessy wanted the young company's headquarters to reflect the vibrancy and dynamism of California, tempered by the tradition and dignity of its French heritage. The structure should complement the site without visually assaulting its neighbors in Yountville or the nearby Veterans' Home. Of course, the winery had to accommodate state-of-the-art equipment and the most advanced techniques in producing sparkling wine. And since the winery would be open to the public, it had to be designed so that visitors could pass through without disturbing production.

ROMA's designers plunged right in. They studied the environment, scouted other wineries in the valley, brainstormed, sketched, and re-sketched. By the end of 1974 they had a preliminary design, but John Wright felt it

wasn't quite right. He suggested the design team take a trip to France to see the caves of Champagne firsthand; perhaps that would provide additional inspiration. It did. After Mountjoy's return from France (where he visited not only the Champagne region, but Paris, Versailles, and Provence as well), his firm submitted the design that M & H finally approved. It was neither a copy of structures in France nor of other wineries in the valley. Instead, it was a synthesis of the spirit of both France and California—just as the wines that would be produced there were destined to become.

The buildings originally planned as part of the complex were the winery itself, the office, and a visitors' center which combined a tasting salon and mini-museum. A series of vaulted roofs formed the major design element. The materials to be used were Douglas fir, weathering steel, glass, and native stone—all of which blended beautifully with the grasses, wildflowers, and oak trees on the property. Together, the site, the design, and the materials promised a stunning facility.

Now came the task of obtaining the necessary permits from the county officials. Together, ROMA and M & H sat through many meetings with the planning commission, whose members, quite understandably, wanted to know how the building and its use would af-

fect the community. To make visualization easier, ROMA presented not just plans and blueprints, but a scale model. Finally, approval to build the winery was won.

BUILDING THE WINERY

In December, 1975 construction began on the 80,000 square-foot winery, with Christensen & Foster of Santa Rosa as general contractors. Here was a five-million dollar structure going up, adjacent to a town with no drug store, no police or fire department, no mail delivery, not even a traffic light. Did it create much excitement? Not a lick.

From ROMA's standpoint, this was the supreme compliment. M & H had maintained a low profile since its entry in the valley and now insisted that its winery blend gently with the surroundings. Thinking back, many people in the area, including those in the wine industry, barely remember seeing the structure go up. If one wished to be up-to-date on the building's progress, a special trip to the site was required.

PRESERVING THE LANDSCAPE

It is not surprising that few noticed the construction activity. The buildings were designed to minimize the impact of their presence in the rural setting. The decision to make the winery a two-story building is a case in point. Not only did this help make optimal use of gravity in certain pumping procedures, it also minimized the building's "footprint" – the area covered by the structure – on the site. And instead of perching the winery high on the hill so that motorists would see it from miles away, ROMA nestled it against the curve of the hill, where it would be less conspicuous.

Hundreds of specimen oaks were scattered over the landscape when construction of the winery started, and only three were lost completing the first phase. Project architect Gabriel remembers the struggle of planning around an old oak no one could bear to lose. It was big and beautiful; unfortunately, it was in the way of the proposed visitors center. Preserving it became a special challenge for the ROMA team. "We finally designed one of the big, curving walls of the building to go around the root ball of that oak tree," says Gabriel. "We couldn't be sure of its size until construction began, so there was no way to draw the wall accurately ahead of time. While that part of the building went up, the roots of the oak were packed in straw and maintained with water and vitamins." The tree survived its ordeal to become a focal point of the tasting salon's patio.

Similarly, the courtyard of the winery office was planned around three existing blue oak trees. "Ultimately, the need to stay outside their foliage drip line gave us the configuration of the courtyard," Gabriel says. ROMA also managed to place the winery's parking lot in a naturally barren area, preventing needless loss of trees.

DAPPLES THE DRAFT HORSE

Those who stopped by the site during construction saw the usual accoutrements of the building trade: cranes and cement mixers, workers in hard hats, wooden beams and steel supports. If they looked closely, they also spotted an anachronism: a large draft horse harnessed to a wooden stone-boat, giving renewed meaning to the term "horse-power."

Owned by Carneros grapegrower René di Rosa, this huge Percheron had to be recruited from his pastoral life to haul rocks from the steep hillsides to the construction site. In its planning stages, the idea seemed to make perfect sense. Stone was needed for the winery's walls, there was plenty to be found on the property (albeit in areas where access was difficult), and using a horse-drawn sled to move it would not scar the hillside as badly as heavy machines. Only one obstacle stood in the way of the plan: Dapples, the horse chosen for the task, had never done a bit of work in his life.

Thus began the education of Dapples, a horse heretofore content to rule over the di Rosa property with two longhorn steers and a sheep for companionship. A 19-year-old woman was hired to train the horse for his new career. Small, blonde and fearless, she stood nose-to-nose with the 1,800-pound animal and convinced him of the pleasures of productivity. After his training, this huge horse took to his work with surprising gusto. He became a familiar sight on the property, proudly putting his strong shoulders into the laden stone-boat. Some people in the community saw the use of Dapples as a bit of misplaced idealism. Nevertheless, the technique did preserve the landscape, a major consideration of both M & H and ROMA.

CASE OF THE DISAPPEARING TANK

If preserving the environment was important to M & H, so was preserving goodwill.

45

This was demonstrated at the Yountville property even before ground was broken for the winery. One of Yountville's landmarks was a large old redwood water tank, located atop a hill on the M & H property in plain view of the town. One October evening in 1973 it disappeared; only the iron hoops which had held the 20-foot wood staves in place were left behind. Next morning, the town was in shock. "It was like coming home and finding your house had disappeared," says ex-mayor Schmitt. "No one could believe that the tank was gone."

M & H had not removed the water tower. Michaela Rodeno, in her position as public relations director for the young company, did her best to battle persistent rumors to the contrary. "The word was out: multinational giant razes landmark," she says. No one ever discovered the culprit, and the consensus is that its irreplaceable redwood boards are now part of someone's chic Marin County home. Rumors were quelled when M & H, at considerable expense, placed a replica of the familiar tank on that same, highly visible knoll. "They couldn't have done a better thing," says Don Schmitt, thinking back. The company's reputation as a good neighbor had been established.

Sometimes, the personal gesture was on a smaller scale. There was the time that earthmoving equipment was rerouted to spare a tiny but sentimentally valuable monument. One member of the early construction crew at Yountville had buried his dog on the hillside. Chip Bouril, then M & H's representative on the building project, knew of the grave. When the heavy machinery headed for the spot, Bouril arranged to divert it and preserve the small stone marker.

MAX
Nov '76
SOME SAY WAS A
DOG
Hit by
A
CAR
ON tHE
NOG

RAISE HIGH THE ROOFBEAMS

Unseasonably dry weather helped speed construction in the winter of 1976. M & H employees were thrilled to see the building take shape and often dropped by to watch the work. As a matter of course, everyone checked in at the construction trailer, parked between what is now the winery office and the visitors center. This was the spot to hear the latest gossip, to grab a hard hat for site visits, to look at the plans and wonder (silently, of course) if M & H would really have its 100,000-case capacity winery finished on schedule, some 18 months down the road.

One early visitor, stopping by to tour the site, remembers thinking what an "imposing chore" lay ahead for the young company. Some four years later, that visitor – David Berkeley of

Corti Brothers in Sacramento, and wine consultant to the Reagan White House – would select sparkling wine made in that very facility to serve at a state dinner honoring the President of France.

For insiders, a single event in 1976 signalled the building's transformation from blueprint to reality: the raising of the first tilt-up wall panels. To make these panels, a special technique had been developed. Stones hauled from the hillsides by Dapples were carefully arranged on a bed of sand in a form, then concrete was poured over them. After curing, the panel could be raised and the excess sand clinging to the rock face washed off. This technique saved more than half the cost of hand-laid rock walls.

When word reached M & H employees that the first panel was ready to be tilted up, they hurried to the site and staked out positions on the hillside. While the giant crane slowly tilted the 60-ton panel upward, the cheering M & H crew toasted the event with Moët. Before long, the 150,000 bottles aging at Trefethen would be ready for drinking, and the people of M & H would be able to toast each other with their own sparkling wine. ——————

48

The bottling room at Domaine Chandon.

When 1976 was rung in, M & H had high hopes that the 150,000 bottles of sparkling wine aging at Trefethen would be ready to sell before year's end. In the meantime, there was work to be done — cuvées to be blended and bottled, grapes to be harvested and pressed, a winery to be finished and outfitted.

The small M & H staff had already outgrown its makeshift headquarters in the garage on Mt. Veeder and moved to Vintage 1870, an office and shopping complex in Yountville. The complex was a restored brick winery and distillery originally called the Groezinger Wine Company. In 1870, its vineyard holdings had included the M & H winery site to the west of town.

Vintage 1870 became the hub of Yountville. If you wanted a bite to eat, you dropped by its restaurant, the Chutney Kitchen. If you wanted to check the latest releases in wine, you paid a call on Phil Faight at Groezinger's Wine Shop. If you wanted more information on the sparkling wines of M & H, you stopped in at the second floor offices of the young company and talked with president Wright, marketing and public relations director Michaela Rodeno, or sales director Stu Harrison. Without much coaxing, any one of them would take you across Route 29 — a three-minute drive, if you obeyed both stop signs — and show you

CHAPTER FIVE

Going Public

the progress at the winery site. Special guests might be invited to Trefethen, where one of the bottles aging would be disgorged and tasted. Understandably, this privilege was reserved for those who understood that, like humans, sparkling wine goes through awkward stages in its journey toward maturity.

One of the first outsiders given this special opportunity was Robert Lawrence Balzer, the same wine writer who had found M & H's modest headquarters on Mt. Veeder in the company's first year of operation. "I arrived at Trefethen about 11 one bright morning," he says. "We went into the lab – John Wright, Edmond Maudière, and I – and John took the wine out of the refrigerator. When it was poured, it seemed to have a slightly perceptible blush, so rather surreptitiously I slipped my glass over a piece of white paper to see for sure. When this confirmed the hint of color, my mind began racing – should I or shouldn't I ask about it? Finally, I blurted out, 'Is the color accidental or deliberate?' That's when Edmond explained that they were having trouble keeping the Pinot Noir from shedding a faint blush of color into the wine."

According to Balzer, Wright was prepared to defend the blush. He referred his guest to a venerable book on the history of champagne by Vizetelly (a book Balzer had in his personal collection and knew well) which tells of similarly-tinted champagnes served in the eighteenth century. "They were known as the lion's mane," says Balzer, "and were very popular in England." If the truth be known, he adds, he didn't really object to the color of the wine he sampled, but was curious about the winemaker's intent. "The wine was so delicious that the color didn't matter," he says.

BY ANY OTHER NAME

From the start, the name "M & H Vineyards" had not appealed to John Wright. So he was not pleased to receive a letter from Moët & Chandon saying, "As far as the brand name is concerned, at present 'M & H' has been indicated." By return mail, Wright wrote back and tactfully aired his feelings on the subject: "I am a little disappointed that 'M & H' is considered the best brand name for our California product, mainly because it is rather undistinguished. So many plumbing companies are named 'M & M' or 'C & B', or similar combinations of letters. I would really prefer to have a brand name that is more in line with the elegance of champagne."

Wright's letter helped clarify what the name should not be, but deciding what it should be was no simple task. From France came the suggestion to use "Claude Moët" as a brand name, in honor of the parent company's founder. Count de Vogüé, whose brainchild M & H had been, also wanted Moët in the new venture's name. Frédéric Chandon suggested the name "Comte Chandon" for the California product. Wright countered with a derivative of that idea. How about "Caveau Chandon," he asked, to recall the *caves*, or storage areas, where sparkling wine ages. When Wright was informed that *caveau* also means "crypt" in French, he shelved the idea.

Finally, someone came up with "Domaine Chandon": *domaine* meaning estate or property, Chandon obviously in homage to the firm's French parentage. The suggestion was well-received, both at M & H and at Moët-Hennessy, but company lawyers had their doubts about its acceptability because of the presence of Almaden's "Le Domaine" sparkling wine on the market. Nevertheless, the new name was registered in early 1976. Trefethen took it on as a fictitious business name for a few months so that the label would indicate that the first bottlings of sparkling wine were "produced and bottled by Domaine Chandon." The name would be transferred back to M & H after sparkling wine operations moved to Yountville.

ALL THAT SPARKLES...

From the first announcement that Moët-Hennessy planned to produce sparkling wine in California, there was speculation about what it would be called. Would the French dare to name their product champagne — flouting the legally defensible tradition that says only sparkling wines made to strict specification in the Champagne region of France can claim that appellation? Certainly — most other American producers had done so. Traditional dry sparkling wines from Korbel, Kornell, and Schramsberg carried the appellation "champagne," modified only to indicate their California origins, and many marketing experts believed it was risky to do otherwise.

John Wright remembers distinctly the first time the wine's appellation was discussed internally. It was soon after the March, 1973 incorporation, and Robert-Jean de Vogüé brought the subject up. "I don't see why the champenois get so upset when others make sparkling wine and call it champagne," de Vogüé declared. "After all, this just recognizes that champagne is the greatest. So John, please don't worry. If you feel you must call your *mousseux* 'champagne,' go ahead and do it!" Only a man with the stature in Champagne of Count de Vogüé would have dared such heresy.

Although Wright was happy to be given free rein, he did not believe that calling the mousseux (the sparkling wine) "champagne" was the right thing to do. His reasoning was

51

simple. French champagne is champagne; what his company planned to make would be California sparkling wine. But since no decision was necessary right away, Wright turned his attention to other matters.

About six months later, Wright read an interview in which a Moët-Hennessy official categorically stated that his company would never put the word champagne on the label of its California product. "There it was in bold print," says Wright. "The decision had been made for me. But even if the article hadn't made this a fait accompli, I suspect we would have come to the same decision. I always felt that having the label say 'Chandon' was a heck of a lot more important than having it say 'champagne.'"

READYING THE FIRST RELEASE

The bottles *en tirage* at Trefethen rested undisturbed for a year and a half, aging on the yeast that Maudière had so carefully nurtured. On a regular basis, Maudière or Domaine Chandon's winemaker Sergio Traverso would open a bottle to check its development, and by the summer of 1976 they had agreed that the cuvées had matured favorably in taste and bouquet. The bottles should be prepared, Maudière said, for riddling—the next step in the traditional méthode champenoise.

In an established champagne cellar, preparation for riddling would be fairly simple. Bottles that had been aging *sur lattes* would be placed, neck down, in wooden riddling racks in a cool area of the cellar. For Domaine Chandon's first bottles, however, the logistics were much more complicated. The bottles sur lattes were on the second floor at Trefethen: the racks in which they would be riddled were to be set up in the partially completed winery in Yountville.

While the construction crew continued to pour a section of concrete at the new winery, workers at Trefethen were loading bottles into bins. The bins were then trucked five miles up Highway 29 to Yountville. As soon as the concrete in a section of the new cellar's floor was cured, Domaine Chandon workers set up riddling racks—some 250 of them, imported from Champagne—and at Maudière's direction, loaded them with the bottles just arrived from Trefethen. Winemaker Traverso then handed the crew cans of pink paint and told them to mark the punt of the first bottles in each row. Though unsure why, they followed his instructions.

"For the first few rows, we painted the marks like big pink tongues," recalls one worker. "Then Sergio stopped us and explained." The marks, they learned, were to serve as guides for those who would be riddling the bottles. For that reason, they should be visible but not overly conspicuous; they would, after all, be washed off before the bottles left the winery for market.

RIDDLE ME THIS

Riddling (or *remuage,* as the French say) is an art reserved for a highly skilled group of cellar workers in the French champagne houses. Basically, the process involves manipulating bottles in a carefully-choreographed series of turns, so that at the end of several weeks the sediment remaining in the sparkling wine after fermentation has been gradually coaxed down into the neck of the bottle. When all the sediment is resting directly next to the crown cap in the plastic plug known as the *bidule,* the entire mass can be "disgorged"—expelled from the bottle—leaving the wine brilliant and free of impurities.

Domaine Chandon arranged to bring over Moët's retired *chef remueur,* head riddler Lucien Dambron, to riddle its first bottles in mid-1976. He was also charged with teaching three apprentices the art he had perfected during his 40-year career. One of the young men selected was Ken de Horton, who would become *chef remueur* of Domaine Chandon. He remembers the first day on the job with Dambron as tense but exciting, the normal confusion of learning a new skill intensified by the fact that the teacher spoke no English and the students no French.

"Lessons" were silent periods of watching and imitating, sometimes facilitated by the translations of winemaker Traverso. With the grace that comes with experience, Dambron would riddle three racks while the apprentices, working as hard as they could, would struggle to finish one. At first, the work was exhausting. A few hours of riddling left the Californians with aching hands, wrists, forearms, and backs. Soon, however, their muscles adapted and they caught the rhythm that good riddlers seem to feel. By the end of their six-week apprenticeship, they were turning 20,000 bottles a day to Dambron's 50,000. Slowly and carefully, they prepared Domaine Chandon's first tirage of 150,000 bottles for disgorgement.

53

When Wright and Maudière explained the process of hand disgorgement to the Domaine Chandon bottling crew, their reaction was a simple "you're kidding." Yes, they could see the sediment nestled in the bidule within the neck of the riddled bottles. But whether it could be expelled in the fashion described—that remained to be seen.

The disgorging process calls for the bottles to be placed neck down in a cold brine solution to trap the sediment in a plug of frozen wine. Next, the bottles are turned upright and their crown caps loosened with a bottle opener. Here's where the fun comes—when the six atmospheres of pressure resulting from fermentation in the sealed bottle propels the sediment-filled bidule (with its casing of frozen wine) out of the bottle, taking the crown cap with it. All this sounded far-fetched to Domaine Chandon's inexperienced bottling line workers, but it was not the first time they had been surprised by a new aspect of the méthode champenoise.

That first hand disgorgement was a stop-and-go circus, overseen by ringmasters Wright, Maudière, and Gino Zepponi, a consultant who later became Domaine Chandon's vice president of operations. It was cold and wet in the unfinished building and few of the shiver-ing workers had rubber boots. One young woman started wearing large plastic garbage bags taped around her legs to keep them dry, until management finally issued boots to everyone. The construction din of hammering and sandblasting made it difficult to talk, but perhaps this was a blessing. The new workers needed to focus all their concentration on the job at hand.

Sometimes, total concentration wasn't enough; the body just refused to continue. When the bottles come out of the brine bath before disgorging, they are freezing cold. Many times, early workers say, hands became numb and bottles slipped, crashing to the floor. "If an open bottle landed on its punt, the wine would gush up like a geyser," says one veteran. "Other times, the bottle would scoot back and forth like a rocket gone crazy from all the pressure being released."

If a bottle blew (and some did), there was usually an accompanying shriek from the person nearest it. "It was an automatic reaction," says a woman who worked on that first disgorging line. "Each time a bottle popped, I would find myself screaming." Despite the cold and the noise and the lack of experience, Domaine Chandon's crew managed to disgorge thousands of bottles each day.

After the sediment has been ejected, a brut *dosage* containing a mixture of reserve wine and sugar is added to each bottle. This, the workers learned, serves to round out or finish the wine. All sparkling wines except those labeled "natural" receive a dosage in varying degrees of sweetness. After this process, the bottles are "topped up" to assure that each has an even fill before being corked, wired, and foiled. At last, the bottles were beginning to look like sparkling wine.

TO MARKET, TO MARKET

While Domaine Chandon's cellar and bottling-line workers were concentrating on the wines, the marketing team was planning strategy. Unlike some young companies, Domaine Chandon's first challenge was not figuring out how to sell what they had made, but how to decide who would get the limited quantities available in the first release. According to the group's best estimates, about 2,000 cases would be ready just before Christmas 1976. The decision was made to limit distribution to California and to assign priority to outlets that could give the new sparkling wine prime exposure during its all-important debut.

Under California's fair trade laws in 1976, producers had to sign a contract with a retailer and file prices with the state before their wines could be sold to the public. Domaine Chandon, from its temporary headquarters at Vintage 1870, entered into its first such agreement with Phil Faight of Groezinger's Wines. Faight remembers the circumstances well. "I got a call from the Domaine Chandon crowd saying they were having a party upstairs. Would I like to come up? Then they told me there was one hitch: I would have to sign my name to this agreement." Faight went upstairs, signed, and thus helped launch Domaine Chandon's commercial venture. It was only fitting. When comparative tastings were held at Domaine Chandon's Vintage 1870 offices, Faight often found the desired bottles in Groezinger's stock downstairs and would obligingly chill them for the tastings. No matter that the only container large enough to accommodate six or eight bottles was his industrial-size mop bucket—complete with wringer and wheels. More than once, it was suggested that Faight should have the Domaine Chandon star logo stencilled on this dual-purpose receptacle.

RACING WITH THE CALENDAR

As the staff of Domaine Chandon knew, it was vital to get the new sparkling wine on the market by Christmas. The holidays are always a peak consumption period for sparkling wine and champagne—too important to miss. That's why Wright and sales director Harrison spent early December fretfully checking in at the winery to see when those first cases would be

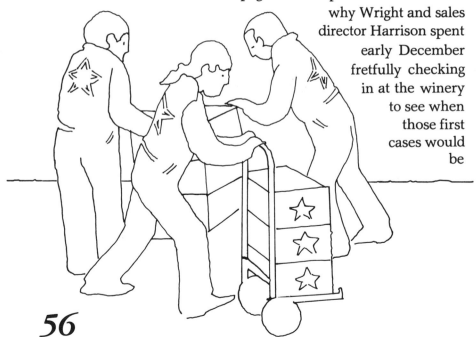

ready. More than once, they helped to hand-foil bottles and struggled to glue on, as Wright calls them, "those damn *collerettes.*" Christmas was coming and it was important that Chandon's Napa Valley Brut be part of the celebration.

When the wine was finally ready to go to market, it did not travel there by the usual means. Instead of using an independent trucking firm, Wright decided to rent five small trucks and enlist several employees to make the deliveries directly from the winery. Outfitted in tan coveralls with the star logo in green on their backs, they loaded the allotted cases and set off to deliver the wine. They had only a few hours to do the job; the annual Domaine Chandon Christmas party was scheduled for that same night.

"We felt like we were leading an invasion," says Harrison, thinking of the moment when the fleet of loaded trucks pulled away from Yountville. "We had even given ourselves CB type 'handles'—Bubbling Bandit or Champagne Charlie, for instance. It was really exciting to know the wine was eagerly awaited."

PRESENTING DOMAINE CHANDON

One of the first stops Harrison made was to drop off five cases of Napa Valley Brut to the London Wine Bar in San Francisco. "We were the first place to have Chandon released on premise in California," remembers owner

John Overall. "It was an immediate and great success—people were dying to taste it. Here was this wonderful American wine wrapped up in a French cloak. Customers could feel as if they were ordering French and drinking American." Harrison was so caught up in Overall's excitement about Domaine Chandon that he drove off without his dolly, and had to return to claim it before he could continue his deliveries. Such were the hazards of "amateur" help.

At that evening's Christmas party, there was much singing and dancing and joke-telling—but that was always the case at Domaine Chandon parties. This time, the celebration had special significance. Employees, many of whom had been with the company since its beginning, were sipping their own creation: Chandon Napa Valley Brut. Like Dom Pérignon, they felt as if they were drinking stars.

58

The flagpoles at Domaine Chandon, with the colors of the United States, France, California, and Champagne.

January 1977 was a busy month for John Wright. The release of Chandon Napa Valley Brut brought a deluge of attention from wholesalers, retailers, and restaurateurs eager to stock the product. Journalists were calling, too, wanting comments on everything from the advisability of foreign investment in California to the state of the American palate. Suddenly, California sparkling wine was hot, just as it had been in 1972, when President Nixon took 13 cases of Jack Davies' Schramsberg Napa Valley Champagne to toast Chou En-lai during his historic visit to China. In 1977, Domaine Chandon was the new kid on the block, and lots of folks were out to sell it, sip it, and sing its praises.

Besides dealing with the trade and the press, Wright was also keeping watch on the Domaine Chandon winery, scheduled for completion in April. Construction was progressing smoothly, but plans for the visitors center had changed somewhat. Originally, it was to house a tasting salon, a mini-museum, a tiny banquet kitchen, and a staging area for tours. After construction began, Wright decided to propose the inclusion of a full-service restaurant to Moët-Hennessy. The beauty of the site had originally given him the idea. "It seemed like a logical step to encourage visitors to stop and spend time here," he says.

The restaurant idea was readily approved by

CHAPTER SIX

Officially at Home

Moët-Hennessy, whose ownership of the Château de Saran proved its commitment to the marriage of food and wine. But getting a permit from Napa County to allow a restaurant as part of the project was not so easy. A series of meetings and hearings was held with public officials, with Michaela Rodeno, responsible for public and community relations, pleading Domaine Chandon's case. Should restaurants, not permitted in agricultural zones, be an acceptable accessory use to wineries, which are permitted? Domaine Chandon stressed the minimal impact of its restaurant in the context of the winery complex, and wondered what harm a beautiful restaurant could do.

Domaine Chandon's first request for a use permit was denied, but the decision was reversed on appeal. The January 12, 1977 issue of the Napa Register carried the headline, "Supervisors Indicate Okay of Dining Hall at Winery." Wright and Rodeno may have chuckled over the reference to their proposed culinary gem as a dining hall, but they were happy with the results. Though some official rezoning remained to be done, the plans for a restaurant could proceed. With luck, it would be ready to open that June, just in time for the influx of summer visitors.

January was also the month that top management from Moët-Hennessy chose to call on the California operation. The retiring president of Moët-Hennessy, Kilian Hennessy, was accompanied by the incoming president, Count Frédéric Chandon de Briailles, and the managing director, Alain Chevalier. They not only toured the new winery, they toured the vineyards at Carneros, Mt. Veeder, and those most recently acquired—a 130-acre parcel in front of the winery site at Yountville. An employee at Carneros recalls one significant detail of that visit. "We offered to drive them in a jeep, but they preferred to walk the vineyards. That, I think, says something about how they feel about the business."

By the time the Moët-Hennessy group had completed its visit, they had toured every square inch of Domaine Chandon and tasted all the cuvées at various stages of development. The consensus was that of proud parents: the child was not without faults, but it was robust and healthy and showed the limitless promise of youth. Domaine Chandon would do its ancestors proud.

A TIME TO CELEBRATE

As April—the month scheduled for the winery's dedication—drew closer, many wondered if it were possible to complete all the work as planned. "It was a madhouse," says Wright, thinking back to those hectic final weeks of construction. Others insist that was an understatement. The entry to the winery was paved the day before the planned opening. That evening, the construction crew stayed late to clean up for the next day's festivities.

The formal dedication was scheduled for April 23, 1977. For many of the Domaine Chandon crew, the "real" dedication had already taken place. The bottling line, which at first had been set up in the riddling area, was finally moved into the spacious, airy room designed to house it permanently. "It was big, fresh, and pretty," a crew member says, "just the place for a party." Renowned organist E. Power Biggs had recently died, so several people decided a memorial celebration for him was in order. Stereos were set up in the big, nearly-empty bottling area, and the departed Biggs was saluted with Chandon sparkling wine. Attendees decided it was unlikely any formal dedication could top this gathering.

The opening festivities took place as scheduled during one whirlwind weekend of events. Those who attended the first event—the dedication of the winery—were greeted at the gatehouse by the sight of four flags flying: those of the United States, France, California, and Champagne. They wound their way up the long, recently paved driveway toward the parking area. A short walk across a footbridge led them into the visitors center, a stone-faced structure seemingly cut into the hillside. Then it was up the stairs, pausing first to look at the display of wine-making objects and artifacts from Champagne, and into the courtyard for the dedication ceremony. The three blue oak trees so carefully preserved by the architects softened the newness of the building.

The winery was to be christened—yacht-launching style—by smashing two magnums (Moët & Chandon Brut Impérial champagne and Chandon Napa Valley Brut sparkling wine) against its walls. The magnums were suspended by cords from an overhanging roof, making the enterprise safer for the dignitaries doing the christening. John Wright started things off. He drew back his magnum of Chandon, released it, and heard it break against the stone wall to enthusiastic applause. Moët-Hennessy's Chevalier had to contend with a tough-skinned magnum of Moët. After bouncing off the wall twice, it finally broke, again to spirited cheers.

Showing the guests through the cellar was next on the agenda, but Wright stole a moment to recount his favorite Portuguese proverb, which summarizes the steps every new organization goes through. "First there's enthusiasm, followed by complication, disillusionment, search for the guilty, castigating the innocent, and honoring those who did nothing," he said. "So far in this venture, we've avoided numbers four and five. This dedication is to honor those who did everything."

Chevalier had his chance to give the Moët-Hennessy viewpoint over a luncheon of *filet de boeuf financière*. "We came here not as investors or industrialists, but as winemakers. We hope that our Napa Valley Brut—which is in our minds neither an imitation nor a competitor of champagne, but a typically Californian product of high quality—will help maintain the prestige of American wines as well as that of our company."

For John Wright, there was one touch of sadness in the dedication: Robert-Jean de Vogüé, who had died in the fall of 1976, was not there to see his dream realized. Several years earlier during a golf game, the count told Wright he did not expect to live to see the operation completed. At the time, the remark seemed odd to the president of the fledging company. At the dedication, it seemed sad.

That evening, after the formal dedication of the winery, another gala party was held to benefit the Presbyterian Hospital of the Pacific Medical Center. Busloads of formally-attired San Francisco socialites spilled into the parking lot and meandered up to the winery, where the party was to be held. While most of the bottling line equipment had been temporarily removed, the *bac à glace*—a large, rectangular unit used to freeze the necks of bottles before disgorging—had been covered with a plywood board to create a bar. It was camouflaged with ficus trees. The huge room offered plenty of space for 400 guests to dine and to dance to a 20-piece orchestra. Chandon Napa Valley Brut flowed in abundance, although it had to compete for attention with a fashion show featuring models in gold bikinis, and favors of Dior perfume. The following day, a huge reception was held for friends and neighbors from the Napa Valley.

GOING PUBLIC

Immediately after this round of private festivities, Domaine Chandon opened its doors to visitors. April 25, 1977 marked the official opening, the first day the public could tour the winery at Yountville. And tour they did—led by one of eight nervous tour guides, who were

giving their 30-minute presentations for the first time.

The tours are one part of Domaine Chandon's program inspired by Moët & Chandon's visitors program in France. In 1976, Michaela Rodeno visited the parent company to gather ideas and to experience its legendary hospitality. Out of her trip came plans for a visitors program. Gwen Rogers, hired several months before its opening to manage the visitors center, made sure each of the guides was well-versed in all aspects of sparkling wine production. For several weeks, guides underwent rigorous training, hearing lectures on everything from history to viticulture. This was no 9 to 5 training program; there were heavy reading assignments and numerous site visits. When the tour guides realized the variety of questions visitors could pose, they were happy for such extensive preparation.

Kurt Horn, a retired Air Force flight instructor, took the first group of visitors through the winery. Years as a teacher stood him in good stead. The tour guide scheduled to lead the second tour saw him returning with his group, all smiles, and was seized with stage fright.

63

Paralyzed, she convinced Kurt to turn around and take the next group, too, until she could pull herself together.

At the conclusion of each tour, the guide returned with his or her group to the visitors center, where they were invited to purchase Chandon sparkling wines in the tasting room, "Le Salon." This was not the usual practice among wineries receiving visitors. Customarily these wineries offered a free taste or two of their wines to those visiting. Although this break with tradition might have been misunderstood, Wright felt it was important to charge for the wines. It would enable Domaine Chandon to provide ample servings in a leisurely setting appropriate to the luxury image of the product. He also counted on the psychological implication of "you get what you pay for." Far from discouraging visitors, the policy met with ready acceptance. The Salon and its adjoining outdoor patio quickly became a favorite gathering place for valley residents and visitors. So relaxing was it that many who had planned a day of touring Napa Valley wineries never made it farther north than Yountville.

THE RESTAURANT OPENS

With the winery finally open to the public, the focus of effort turned to the restaurant. A full-service kitchen had not been part of the architects' original design, and it was too late to redesign the entire building. That meant the kitchen was located beneath the dining area, and food would have to be transferred upstairs via dumb-waiters. It wasn't ideal, but it would do for the time being.

For the dedication ceremonies in April, Moët & Chandon had loaned Domaine Chandon the executive chef of its private dining facility in Epernay, Joseph Thuet. His knowledge of the use of champagne both in cooking and as an accompaniment to meals was valuable in planning menus. When the restaurant finally opened in June, 1977, it was under the supervision of *chef de cuisine* Udo Nechutnys, a protégé of Paul Bocuse and a proponent of his mentor's lighter style of preparing classic dishes. To assist him, he had *chef saucier* Philippe Jeanty, a young chef who had worked three years under Thuet at Moët & Chandon. Their plan was to serve an elegant buffet at lunch and provide a la carte selections for dinner. In the evening, restaurant guests could sip aperitifs by the fireside while making their selections.

Within weeks of the restaurant's opening, reservations were already hard to come by. The luncheon buffet quickly became the talk of the valley—with its elaborate spun sugar and ice sculptures, its array of hot and cold dishes, and its dessert table laden with delights from *crème bavaroise* to petits fours. The dinner menu featured dishes created to showcase the excellent local products. Naturally, Domaine Chandon sparkling wines were available to accompany lunch or dinner, by the bottle or by the glass. Although, at first, California law prevented the restaurant from selling wines produced by other wineries, patrons were encouraged to bring their own bottles. Domaine Chandon's policy has always been to encourage the use of wine with meals, so there was only a small corkage fee.

A BRIEF APPRENTICESHIP

This modest corkage fee caused a small problem for John Wright. In an effort to "get the feel" of the place, he was working as a waiter in the new restaurant, handling two tables at dinner. A well-dressed couple at one of his tables had brought along a half bottle of Chateau Lafite '61 to drink with their meal. Wright decanted and served it, happy to see the fine wine enjoyed with Domaine Chandon's cuisine.

Later, after the couple's bill had been presented, the man called Wright over to the table. "Waiter, there's a problem with the bill. You charged me too much for corkage." Wright re-examined his figures, but found nothing amiss. "This is correct, sir," he told the man. "It's $1.50 a bottle for corkage." The man looked puzzled. "That's just what I mean," he said. "If you'll remember, we had only a half bottle." At that moment, Wright realized that the restaurant business would be anything but predictable – not unlike the business of making sparkling wine.

66

A view of the restaurant at Domaine Chandon.

CHAPTER SEVEN

Coming of Age

*F*ew people know that Moët-Hennessy's original plan for Domaine Chandon called for the company to produce sparkling wines by the transfer process as well as by the more complex méthode champenoise. The idea was to use the méthode champenoise for about 250,000 bottles out of every 100,000 cases produced. The rest would be made by the transfer method, which eliminates the costly riddling and disgorging processes.

From the French point of view, this was the most practical route. Knowing from their own experience how difficult riddling can be, they felt it would be impossible for Domaine Chandon to riddle more than 250,000 bottles a year with any certainty or regularity and that this would limit production of wines made by the méthode champenoise. John Wright didn't agree. "I believed that if Moët could riddle 20 million bottles a year, we certainly could do more than 250,000. But I didn't object to the strategy of starting out with méthode champenoise and switching later to transfer. Frankly, I was convinced that once we launched a product made in the traditional way, no one would have the nerve to switch over."

Wright's hunch was correct. After the first riddling was completed in 1976 – "and went pretty well," he adds – the issue of production by transfer method was politely forgotten. Everyone at Domaine Chandon was happy with the decision, but it had come a bit late to be factored into the winery's design. No one had figured on needing space to riddle more than the 250,000 bottles originally suggested, so the *cave* had not been designed large enough. Scarcely a year after the first part of the winery was completed, plans for a second-phase expansion were accelerated.

SETTLING IN

As the thrill of moving into the new winery subsided, Domaine Chandon workers began to realize that for the moment they were working with machinery that was well below state-of-the-art. Much of it came from the parent company in France, and some pieces of equipment qualified for "antique" status. "It was hardly efficient, but at those first low levels of production it made sense," explains John Wright. "To keep down our total costs, we made a conscious decision to start as a semi-automatic hand operation. And that meant using lots of obsolete machines and lots of elbow grease."

One of those obsolete machines was an old corker/wire hooder bought over from Epernay. Every time a bottle fed through it, there was a terrible racket. "We affectionately dubbed it the clunker-chunker," one bottling line worker says. "You simply couldn't hear yourself think when it was running." Not all the noise, however, came from the machines. Prior to *pointage*—loading bottles in the riddling racks—bottles are given a shaking to dislodge the sediment from their inner walls. To combat boredom during this monotonous chore, cellar workers began to cluck, crow, and ham it up in imitation of a "funky chicken" as they strutted to the racks, flexing their elbows to shake the bottles. They became so boisterous during this once-dull maneuver that the tour guides, hard-pressed to explain their strange behavior to visitors, finally asked them to calm down.

Supervising this less-than-conventional operation was Gino Zepponi, vice-president of winery operations. An engineer, consultant, and partner with Norman de Leuze in ZD Winery, Zepponi has an eclectic background. He joined Domaine Chandon in 1976, first as a consultant and later full-time. "If he hadn't come in, we would have all been in trouble," says Wright. "Gino has the amazing ability to combine the strengths of a highly creative engineer with the sensible viewpoints of a production manager." Both sides of Zepponi's talent were challenged by the start-up period in the new building.

AUTOMATIC RIDDLING

One of the problems Zepponi turned his attention to in 1980 was that of riddling, the hand process which he then regarded as "the bottleneck of the operation." If Domaine Chandon was to produce its ambitious goal of 400,000 cases by 1985, Zepponi knew that some form of automatic riddling must be perfected. Thus it was that experimentation began with *gyropalettes*, French machines capable of simulating the series of twists and turns that

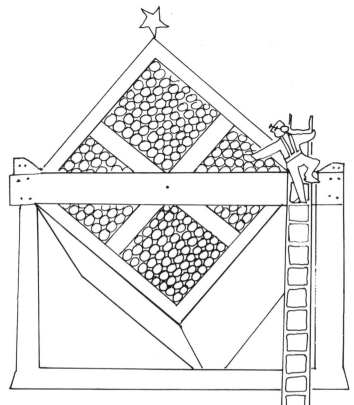

human riddlers put their bottles through by hand. The gyropalette, an invention of Frenchman Pierre Martin, could manipulate 504 bottles simultaneously. "Plus it could work seven day weeks," Zepponi points out, "and it didn't want holidays and weekends off." It could not, however, make a judgment about how best to riddle a particular cuvée, a decision "remueurs" learn to make through experience and close observation. Therein lay the problem: how to combine the gyropalette's capacity for work with the riddler's capacity for decision-making.

Zepponi started by purchasing a single gyropalette. The bottles riddled by this machine were tested, and found to be as clear

69

as (or clearer than) those riddled by hand. Of course, an experienced riddler was deciding exactly how the bottles should be turned; the art of riddling had not been forgotten, only mechanized.

But Zepponi was not yet satisfied with this part of the operation, mainly because the gyropalette, designed for the low caves of French champagne houses, did not efficiently utilize the space in Domaine Chandon's high-ceilinged cellar. After several experiments, he finally developed a prototype gyropalette 17 feet high, capable of riddling 4,032 bottles simultaneously – eight times more bottles than the original design. To control its movements, he came up with the concept of a computer liaison, which he commissioned a small electronics firm to develop.

Still, it remained to find a way to direct the day-to-day operation of the large gyropalettes. Since different batches of bottles required different treatment, no single control program would be appropriate in every case. Solution? Domaine Chandon chose Jim Doescher, one of its experienced riddlers who had trained with Lucien Dambron, to examine bottles scheduled for automatic riddling and to program the proper moves into the gyropalette's computer. Tests showed the results were exceptional. Wright and Zepponi decided to automate the bulk of the riddling operation. Hand riddling would

also be continued under the direction of Ken de Horton.

The redesigned automatic riddler was really no longer a little gyropalette; clearly, it needed another name. The cellar crew took to calling it the "VLM" – for Very Large Machine – when Zepponi was away in Europe. When he returned, the cellar workers didn't bother to explain the new name, but simply mentioned the VLM in a weekly meeting. As Doescher remembers it, Zepponi hardly missed a beat. He knew his staff called the 1,000 hectoliter fermentation tanks VLT's (for Very Large Tanks); what else could they be speaking of when they said VLM but his invention, the Very Large Machine?

Production techniques weren't the only things undergoing change at Domaine Chandon. A new winemaker, Dawnine Sample Dyer, assumed the day-to-day responsibilities of overseeing production of the company's sparkling wines following the resignation of Sergio Traverso. She had worked at the winery since the harvest of 1976 and had an unusually strong laboratory background. "From the start, it was very easy working with Dawnine," remembers consulting enologist Edmond Maudière. "She's a very talented woman."

In the Domaine Chandon restaurant, chef saucier Philippe Jeaunty had been promoted to chef de cuisine in 1978, and he brought his own distinctive culinary style to the menu. The elaborate luncheon buffet had been replaced by à la carte service when the county board of health insisted that a "sneeze guard" be installed for hygienic purposes. No one felt the buffet should be subjected to this aesthetic atrocity, hence its demise.

The office staff continued to grow in order to support the increasingly sophisticated needs of the young company. John Wright, who had resisted having his own office ("preferring to keep his headquarters between his ears," one astute observer notes), was eventually persuaded that a company president should have a private office. He set up shop in what was originally to be the Domaine Chandon conference room, and made the seven-foot round conference table his desk. From this vantage point he could look out a large picture window to the eastern hills of Napa Valley or scribble furiously on the blackboards lining the walls.

The company's speedy growth brought on a combination of exhilaration and tension. From the first day of its release, the sparkling wine was in great demand, making life a tightrope walk for those responsible for sales or marketing. Start-up expenses were high, and Wright knew it would be several years before the company could show a profit. The disorder of never-ending construction was beginning to grate on the nerves of many who worked at

71

critics were helpful. Robert Finigan, Nathan Chroman, Frank Prial, and Robert Lawrence Balzer mentioned the new sparkling wine in their columns, and consumers who read their comments often made a trip to the local wine shop to ask for Chandon. Thinking back, Frank Prial of The New York Times remembers his first reaction to news of the debut of Chandon: "Great idea! It represented a marriage of French experience with American needs. It was an idea that was right for the times."

IT PAYS TO ADVERTISE

Perhaps Chandon was right for the times, but part of the challenge of marketing it lay in convincing people that any time was right for sparkling wine. Historically, Americans considered beverages that bubbled suitable only for special occasions: weddings, New Year's, other festive celebrations. Domaine Chandon wanted to convey the message that its Napa Valley Brut and Blanc de Noirs could be sipped on regular as well as red-letter days. How to get the word out? The decision was made to advertise. (Blanc de Noirs was the new name given to Cuvée de Pinot Noir once it was discovered that some consumers thought Cuvée de Pinot Noir signified sparkling red Burgundy.)

John Wright and Michaela Rodeno realized they needed an agency and set about finding one. Interviews were held with several – large and small, funky and more traditional – but both Wright and Rodeno leaned toward San Francisco's Maxwell Arnold agency, a small, informal shop. During the winnowing out process, principals from this agency were invited to Yountville for a look around the winery. Upon arrival, they were told to meet Wright and Rodeno in the working tasting room.

"At the time, we thought it was the acid test," says Bud Arnold, the agency's president. "We had walked into a blind tasting of Korbel, Schramsberg, Chandon, and Moët. I decided to give it my best shot, and it turned out I ranked Domaine Chandon first." In truth, Wright had simply thought the agency people would enjoy a tasting; it was certainly not a test. But when the final selection was made, Maxwell Arnold (today Maxwell Arnold, Jackson & Smyth) had also been rated number one.

The campaign the agency eventually created revolved around the theme lines of "morning star" and "evening star", referring to the differing appeals of Domaine Chandon's Blanc de Noirs and Napa Valley Brut. Elegant line drawings accompanied sophisticated copy, noting that Brut was suitable "for an evening more than an event" and that its sister product could be sipped "before lunch as well as with it." The ads broke in November, 1978 in The New Yorker, Newsweek, and Los Angeles Magazine. Later, advertising was discontinued for a while; the company did not want to create more demand than it could supply.

The agency was also called upon to help Domaine Chandon with a different marketing problem: how to help the public find the winery in Yountville. Thanks to ROMA's superior job in making the structure unobtrusive, would-be visitors often had difficulty locating the site. Napa County's strict sign ordinance prevented Domaine Chandon from erecting a large sign. Had it not been for the restaurant, an invaluable drawing card, the multi-million dollar winery might have been emptier still.

Brainstorming sessions on the problem yielded several ideas, says Bud Arnold. One involved hoisting a balloon aloft to help visitors spot the winery site from the highway. This would be no ordinary balloon, however. Fashioned to resemble a cork, it would be promoted in ads and billboards exhorting people to "Look for the flying cork!" In the end, a more reserved approach was chosen. One tasteful sign was added near the highway, and an ad—making tongue-in-cheek reference to "French lessons in Yountville"—was placed in several magazines.

ONE MILLION BOTTLES

New markets, enthusiastic critics, an ex- panding and easier-to-find facility. All these factors helped Domaine Chandon sell one million bottles by 1979. For all those involved with the company, this was a milestone to be celebrated. To a select group of "oldtimers," the million-bottle mark held an added significance.

The story goes that on an early visit to California, Count Frédéric Chandon de Briailles, who was to become president of Moët-Hennessy after Kilian Hennessy's retirement, made a promise to employees present at a festive lunch in his honor. "When you sell the millionth bottle of Chandon, I will charter a plane and fly you all to Champagne as my guests," Chandon was purported to have said. A small coterie of veteran workers did not forget the pledge.

At first, however, it seemed to them that Count Chandon had forgotten. The millionth bottle was long sold, but still no word of the trip. Some had already written it off when Chandon came for another visit to California early in 1982. If the subject was ever going to be broached, now was the time. Marcy Thomas, the bottling line supervisor, volunteered for the task of composing a letter which would gently remind Count Chandon of his promise. Her plan was to have the letter delivered to John Wright during a management luncheon at which the count would be present. Should Wright want to let its contents be known, it would be appreciated. If not, the matter would be quietly forgotten.

The day of the luncheon, the entire winery was abuzz. Would John Wright share the letter with the count? Would it be well-received? Would the count be angry, or would he find the situation amusing? Great hopes were riding on his reaction. The letter, borne on a tray by a nervous waitress, was presented to Wright over coffee. He read it, chuckled a bit, and finally read it aloud to Count Chandon. When the count heard the message, he immediately asked to meet Marcy. John Wright took him to her office in the winery, where the count called her "a pioneer of the company" and said yes, she and her cohorts would have their trip as promised.

After meticulously checking records to determine which employees had been with

Domaine Chandon at the time the original promise was made, a list of those eligible for the trip was compiled. The journey was scheduled for October, 1982, with an itinerary that took the group to Paris, Epernay, and Orléans, home of Dior perfumes. The red carpet was rolled out everywhere. There was an elegant dinner at Le Trianon, Moët & Chandon's beautiful dining room in Epernay, with Fred Chandon as host. There was a festive night on the town at the Lido in Paris, complete with magnums of Dom Pérignon, not to mention numerous visits to glass manufacturers, cork producers, and champagne houses – often to see their bottling lines. The count's promise had been fulfilled many times over by journey's end.

When employees speak of the trip, many mention the bond of camaraderie they felt when they saw their counterparts at Moët & Chandon. Certainly there was the language barrier to contend with, and the initial shock when the Californians realized that work clothes in Epernay were shirts and ties or dresses and heels – not jeans and boots. Despite these differences, one similarity provided a link. Like those from Domaine Chandon, the employees of Moët & Chandon knew they weren't just making wine, they were making magic. And the knowledge of this gave the two groups a special kinship.

The truck from which cases of Fred's Friends were sold.

For those new to the world of sparkling wine, one of the hardest lessons to learn is the need for patience. It was not easy for Domaine Chandon employees to come to grips with this in their first seasons of operation; they all wanted something to show for their labors immediately, not three years down the road. Out of this eagerness (and the availability of plenty of press juice) came the idea for two wines: one a crisp, highly-drinkable still wine, the other a refreshing apéritif. Both were modeled on products historically made by the champenois from their press wine, and both were good enough to warrant continuation once the main event, the sparkling wine, came on the market.

CHAPTER EIGHT

With a Little Panache

USING WHAT'S LEFT

When grapes are pressed for Domaine Chandon, the free run juice, or *vin de cuvée*, is kept separate to make the sparkling wine cuvée. This is juice of the highest quality, extracted as a result of the first light pressing of Chardonnay, Pinot Noir, or Pinot Blanc grapes. For every ton of grapes, this amounts to about 100 gallons of juice.

Subsequent pressings yield "cuts" which are slightly lower in sugar and acidity and higher in astringency than the gently pressed vin de cuvée. The first cut, or *première taille,* accounts for about 30 gallons of juice per ton, and the second, the *deuxième taille,* for about 20 gallons more. Upon the recommendation of consulting enologist Edmond Maudière, the tailles of those early crushes at Trefethen were blended to make M & H's first still wine: a crisp Chardonnay, fresh in taste and low in alcohol. It was fermented dry in the style of *Côteaux Champenois,* the "press wine" of the Champagne region.

When this first still wine was being bottled, a question arose as what to call it. Michaela Rodeno's sense of whimsy led her to ask, "Why not 'Fred's Friends'?"—the Fred being none other than Moët-Hennessy president Count Frédéric Chandon de Briailles. John Wright liked the idea, as did the good-humored count. It is rumored that when asked if he objected, he said, "Of course not. But I do expect a royalty."

The first bottling of Fred's Friends—sporting a label hand-stenciled by Rodeno—was meant solely for the enjoyment of Domaine Chandon employees and friends. It was distributed out of Trefethen winery, where it had been fermented and bottled; no barrel aging took place. Perhaps because limited quantities made it something of a rarity, Fred's Friends soon became "the" wine for informal sipping in the area. "It was suddenly chic in the Napa Valley to have Fred's Friends," Edmond Maudière recalls, still slightly incredulous about its success. "It was fashionable, and yes, it was *very* chic."

In California, word of things chic travels fast. So it was that the next time Domaine Chandon bottled Fred's Friends, in 1976, demand was up sharply for the limited offering. Customers paid for the wine in advance (the princely sum of $18.00 a case) and were instructed to collect their prepaid orders at a designated hour near the railroad spur at the Yountville winery site. The back of a flat-bed truck parked on the property was to serve as the pick-up point.

On the appointed day, a mob descended upon the site. Word was out that Fred's Friends was available, and few cared that only those who had paid in advance were supposed to get the wine. One employee filling orders that day remembers the excitement. "All sorts of folks were coming up and saying, 'Hey, remember me?' Everyone wanted the wine as a kind of conversation piece. They were even driving up from San Jose to get it!"

Domaine Chandon continued to make its press wines, adding a still Pinot Noir Blanc to its repertoire in 1977. That same year, the bottlings were given a spiffy new label, featuring a beautifully-tinted drawing of two nubile young women. The drawing was in the art nouveau style of the turn-of-the-century artist Alphonse Mucha; fittingly, the women were lovely enough to warrant the attentions of a count. In 1978, the first year Fred's Friends was made available to the trade, the Pinot Noir Blanc received a gold medal at the Los Angeles County Fair.

THE APPEAL OF PANACHE

If Fred's Friends was born of impatience, it might be said that "Panache" – another product Domaine Chandon makes from its press juices – was born of nostalgia. In this case it was Moët enologist Edmond Maudière's nostalgia for the apéritif called *Ratafia de Champagne* which his grandfather made. "Every year he made a barrelful of Ratafia for our friends and family and every year it was gone after the harvest," Maudière says. "Tasting it as a child is one of my fondest sensory memories." One can imagine why. Essentially Pinot Noir grape juice fortified with pure spirits, Ratafia de Champagne manages to be sweet but not cloying, fruity but not flowery.

John Wright had discovered the special appeal of Ratafia on his many trips to Epernay, and he agreed with his French-born consultant that Domaine Chandon should make a batch. Certainly, they had the main ingredient: Pinot Noir grape juice from the deuxième taille, with all the intensity of color, body, and fruit it should possess for this particular use. What they didn't have was a pure, high-proof alcohol source to fortify the juice and stop its fermentation. Wright tried one batch with vodka, but

admittedly it was awful.

After this fiasco, Wright and Maudière decided that "white lightning" – pure grain alcohol with no flavor characteristics at all – was needed to create a good Ratafia. Unfortunately, it is not sold in California. Since John Trefethen was preparing for a trip to Nevada, a state that does sell the product, he was enlisted to bring back several cases in his private plane.

Trefethen remembers marching into Dart Discount Liquors in Lake Tahoe and asking for four cases of white lightning. "The clerk looked a little surprised," he said. When the man behind the counter recovered his composure, he asked Trefethen what brand. "It really doesn't matter, I'll take all of whatever you've got," Trefethen said. The clerk surmised he was dealing with a desperate character.

As John Trefethen was loading his purchase into the car, he happened to look more closely at the cases. They were marked "Caution, Highly Flammable!" in large letters. Then and there, he reconsidered his offer to fly the alcohol back to the valley in his airplane. But it was difficult finding another mode of transportation for the load (not unwisely, his mother-in-law rejected the suggestion she haul the cargo in her station wagon) and Trefethen ended up flying the cases home as planned. There, the alcohol was blended with the reserved grape juice in a 50-gallon stainless steel barrel. After a

81

bit of aging, Domaine Chandon had its first Ratafia.

When the decision was made to market the product commercially, the Bureau of Alcohol, Tobacco, and Firearms vetoed the company's original plan to call the product "Ratafia," insisting the name was reserved for its kindred product from France. Again a new name was needed and again the idea came from a Rodeno. This time, it was Michaela's lawyer husband, Gregory, who came up with the winning entry. At his suggestion, Domaine Chandon's Ratafia would be called "Panache."

PANACHE GOES PUBLIC

Panache went on the market in 1977. Classified as an apéritif, a category of which the American consumer is still wary, the product was not walking off the shelves. Many Americans, Domaine Chandon discovered, still associated the word "apéritif" with a bitter medicinal flavor, characteristic of many beverages in the category. It would take some persuading to convince the market that Panache tasted like Pinot Noir grape juice — with a sophisticated punch.

Sometimes, the frustration of explaining yet again the characteristics of Panache gave way to mischief. Michaela Rodeno and Domaine Chandon sales representative Bill Teed were at the Monterey Wine Festival when they

came to the end of their tether. A grossly overweight woman approached the display where they were pouring tastes of Blanc de Noirs and Panache to inquire about the product. "What is this stuff 'Panache'?" she asked. "Is it good? Is it sweet? Is it fattening?" she demanded, never once stopping to let an answer be given.

Bill Teed, an extremely slender man, paused a moment before giving his answer. "Let me put it this way, madame," he said. "Three years ago I weighed 300 pounds, but that was *before* I went on the Panache diet!" Mere mention of this incident today brings a smile to Domaine Chandon employees, perhaps because it demonstrates how a potentially unpleasant confrontation can be avoided with a little panache.

The annual Domaine Chandon 10K Vineyard Run.

Companies, like people, develop their own personalities. Appropriately enough, Domaine Chandon is a sparkler – outgoing, community-minded, always up for a party. Perhaps this kind of gregariousness is natural for a company that makes sparkling wine, a drink perennially associated with good humor. After all, as John Wright has been known to say, "Burgundy makes you think silly things. Bordeaux makes you say silly things. But champagne – champagne makes you *do* silly things."

CHAPTER NINE

Ten Years of Sparkle

CELEBRATIONS FOR INSIDERS

Back when the group was known as M & H Vineyards, their parties were often spur-of-the-moment events. If there was no Moët on hand, then beer was an acceptable substitute. Food might be hamburgers and corn grilled in the husks, or a bowl of John Wright's famous *fejoida*. And always there was music – often of the foot-stomping, hand-clapping variety.

When the group moved to Yountville, its partying style changed. Impromptu gatherings were less frequent, but certainly not unheard of. Tour guides, who pooled their tips from generous patrons in the Salon, often met at a local restaurant for an after-hours session to unwind. Those in the office weren't beyond opening a bottle or two of Brut late on Friday afternoon, or heading over to the Salon to watch the sun set and share a flûte of sparkling wine. As the company grew bigger, group gatherings were saved for special occasions, Christmas and the end of crush being the most common.

The end of crush, when grapes from the vineyards have all been harvested and pressed, is just cause for celebration. Makers of sparkling wine have to race rising sugar levels as summer draws to a close, so there's always pressure to harvest and press grapes quickly. But not too quickly, experienced workers warn. Perhaps that's why they once posted a sign in the press area warning "STATUTORY GRAPE: Any grape picked below 18° Brix."

Crush parties at Domaine Chandon are family affairs. Different menus have been tried, from *cioppino* to a prize hog barbecued in a spicy, Panache-based sauce. The barbecued hog may well become a tradition; vice president of viticultural operations Will Nord has managed to buy the Napa Fair's grand champion hog for the party for several years running. Barbecued pig with Blanc de Noirs is beginning to be part of the post-crush ritual, like playing softball and drinking a bit too much.

OPEN INVITATIONS

Now that Domaine Chandon is a public place, many of its celebrations are public, too.

This results from a conscious decision when the company was young to make the Yountville complex a community center. Visitors center director Gwen Rogers puts it this way: "We have lots of important visitors from all around the world. But first and foremost, Domaine Chandon is a local business."

Art exhibits, concerts, and fashion shows have been held here, as have costumed

Renaissance fairs, hot-air balloon races, and auctions whose proceeds go to save the endangered steelhead trout. Special New Year's Eve and Thanksgiving dinners are scheduled annually.

The beauty of the winery and its setting makes it a favorite place for charity events. Many have been held since Domaine Chandon opened, but the Grand Masked Ball for Mardi Gras in 1978 was perhaps the most memorable. For dancing, there was the music of the five-piece Latin band, "Viva Brasil." For class, there was the presence of Brazilian Consul Raul de Smandeck. And for fun, there were the costumes of John Wright and his wife, Renate, who came outfitted as bottles of Chandon Napa Valley Brut and Blanc de Noirs, respectively.

A tradition launched in 1978 was the celebration of Bastille Day at Domaine Chandon, an appropriate salute to the company's French heritage. Francophiles, as well as those lured by the promise of a free flûte of sparkling wine, sometimes storm the winery with a gusto rivaling that of the Parisian mob that stormed the Bastille. Music and entertainment are part of the event; so are costumed tour guides. Visitors seem to enjoy learning the finer points of the méthode champenoise from guides dressed as the Statue of Liberty, the Blue Nun, or even Dom Pérignon himself.

Another Domaine Chandon tradition, begun in 1979, is the 10-kilometer "Run in the Vineyard." Billed as a "semi-serious race," the competition takes place on a course that winds through the vineyard adjacent to Domaine Chandon. It attracts runners of all ages and degrees of dedication, including many Chandon employees. Post-race refreshments give added incentive to keep up the pace.

87

For some employees, the 10-K race conjures up memories of another competition: the foot-race up Mt. Veeder in 1973. Unlike the 10-K run, this was a private affair; only four competitors were involved, each linked in some way to the new company. Mt. Veeder Road is gruelingly steep, and soon participants either dropped out or were questioning their sanity for continuing. This "affair of macho," as one M & H employee dubbed it, had a close finish, but winemaker Kim Giles did reach the top before his closest competitor, avant-garde photographer and field worker Mike Kleinschmidt. Alas, even the winner's thunder was stolen by the female cyclist who streaked across the finish line to win a bet—and a case of Coors.

THE WINEMAKERS AND THE JET

By the summer of 1979, Domaine Chandon had come a long way from those festivities on Mt. Veeder. Proof positive: For a trip to promote sparkling wines, Moët-Hennessy loaned the young subsidiary its Falcon 10 jet, one of the fastest corporate planes in the world at the time. Michaela Rodeno scheduled a special jet tour for six Napa Valley winemakers. Domaine Chandon's consulting enologist Ed-

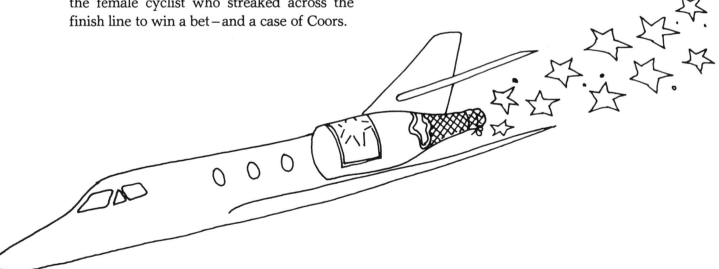

mond Maudière, John Trefethen of Trefethen Vineyards, Jerry Luper of Chateau Montelena, and Francis Mahoney of Carneros Creek Winery went on both legs of the trip. In certain cities, the Louis M. Martini Winery, the Robert Mondavi Winery, and Burgess Cellars were also represented.

Although the pace was breakneck, the winemakers enjoyed their seven-city tour of America in the Moët jet. In Portland, Seattle, Chicago, Boston, Dallas, Houston, and St. Louis the press and public turned out in impressive numbers. In each city, the winemakers participated in a press conference, a seminar for members of the trade, and a tasting for the community (admission, an intended bargain at $5.00). In Chicago, the public tasting drew overflow crowds—an estimated 700 in a banquet room set up for 500 people. Obviously, people were eager to learn more about California wines, and what better teachers than the people who made them?

Edmond Maudière remembers that during the tour he was asked a lot of interesting questions. However, one common query he quickly tired of was, "Which wine do you like better, the Brut or the Blanc de Noirs?" He formulated an answer that was sincere and telling. "The two wines are like my children—both different, both special. And as with children, you don't have to have a preference."

The winemakers' tour helped introduce a large number of people to the Chandon sparkling wines. Another goal of the company was to expose its wines in greater depth to a select group of influential writers and educators. Knowledgeable people all, this group of aficionados already had an appreciation of sparkling wines. But it would be interesting, it was decided, to let them try their hand at blending a cuvée.

"Blend Your Own Cuvée" events were staged for a number of groups in the early eighties, including wine writers in the San Francisco Bay area, Southern California, and New York. Participants were given four ingredients for blending in their own graduated glass cylinders: a Chardonnay, a Pinot Noir, a Pinot Blanc, and a reserve wine from Domaine Chandon's previous year's curvée. They were instructed to strive for a blend that would grow better with age and ultimately yield a good sparkling wine. When they had finished they were given a sample of Maudière's blend from the same ingredients, along with its percentage breakdown. For most, making the comparison was an illuminating experience.

Maudière confesses he can sympathize when knowledgeable people have difficulty creating an appropriate blend. Coming from a long line of champagne-makers, he remembers hearing a discussion between his father and grandfather when he was very young. "They were discussing a cuvée that had not aged as they had hoped. My father said, 'It was *too* good when we blended it! Too rich, too full, too round!'" Wine writers who went through the blending exercise now have even more respect for those like Edmond Maudière and his ancestors who know when a blend is either too good...or not yet good enough.

SALUT

The ultimate test of whether a sparkling wine is "good enough" comes when its cork pops and it is poured. And by 1983, Domaine Chandon's 10th anniversary, some 7,000,000 bottles of its wines had been opened and enjoyed. Most had been drunk without fanfare, but some made headlines. It was usually due to the prestigious positions of those who enjoyed them, as when President Reagan drank Chandon Napa Valley Brut at the Senate luncheon honoring his inauguration, or when President Anwar Sadat sipped Chandon Blanc de Noirs at a state dinner in Washington on August 5, 1981.

The recommendation of the Blanc de Noirs for the Sadat dinner was made by David Berkeley of Corti Brothers in Sacramento, California. As wine advisor to the Reagan White House, Berkeley has had the opportunity to suggest serving Domaine Chandon Napa Valley Brut as well as the Blanc de Noirs. He notes that "Mrs. Reagan seems to love light, colorful desserts in the summer, and the Blanc de Noirs goes especially well with them. At the Sadat dinner, the Blanc de Noirs was served with the final course, a fresh peach *mousse cardinale*."

When planning wines for the state dinner in honor of the Bicentennial Celebration of the Battle of Yorktown, Berkeley suggested Domaine Chandon Special Reserve magnums be poured before the meal. The occasion, with French President Mitterand as the Reagans' guest of honor, was designed to acknowledge the strength of the Franco-American friendship dating from the Revolutionary War period. Chandon, with its unusual dual citizenship, was the perfect toast.

The dinner was held October 18, 1981, at the Governor's Palace in Williamsburg, Virginia. Though not a Republican, John Wright had received an invitation. Delayed in finding his way to the Governor's Palace, he was the last person through the receiving line before the official festivities got underway. He did, however, have the chance to see his wine poured in the candlelit palace, served with small bay oysters and Smithfield ham biscuits. In this opulent setting, it took a wine with star

quality to fit the occasion. Chandon, he decided, had just the sparkle required.

A view of the Domaine Chandon winery.

Epilogue

"Part of the charm of Domaine Chandon is its fluidity and flexibility, its willingness to explore alternatives. Ideas don't get squelched by being run through the corporate hopper."

So says Dr. Barry Stein, a management consultant at the firm of Goodmeasure, Inc. in Cambridge, Massachusetts. Having worked as a consultant for Domaine Chandon, he has an insider's perspective. Interestingly, people coming in contact with the company for the first time often get a similar impression.

The reason is simple. When John Wright launched the venture, it was with a group of enthusiastic amateurs whose ignorance of winemaking kept them from being limited by job descriptions or from accepting the wine world's conventional wisdom. To this group, he added enough qualified professionals to prevent outright chaos. The result was a non-traditional approach to the challenges of a traditional industry – agriculture. This approach was not always the right one, but every now and then it led Domaine Chandon to a break-through in winemaking and in the management of its human resources.

Ten years ago, Domaine Chandon was just a gleam in Robert-Jean de Vogüé's eye. Today, it is people, and a place, and a group of products. All three aspects share a star quality that attracts attention and gives the company its special personality.

The most exciting time to follow stars is when they are on the rise. Such is the case with Domaine Chandon, a company worth watching as it celebrates its first decade of sparkle.

☆ Place a napkin or towel over the bottle to prevent an unplanned cork departure.

☆ Unwind and remove the wire hood. Try not to damage the metallic foil below the hood —it is part of the presentation.

☆ Grasp the cork (still covered with a napkin) in one hand and the bottle in the other. Tilting the bottle away from you and others at a 45 degree angle, slowly twist the bottle—*not* the cork.

☆ As you turn the bottle, the pressure of the bubbles will start pushing the cork out. Keep a firm grip on the cork and gently let it ease itself out. When you hear a little "sigh" of escaping gas, the bottle is open.

☆ Wipe the brim, but avoid wrapping the bottle in a towel for service. Why hide the label when most people prefer to know what is being offered?

☆ Pour a little sparkling wine in each glass... then fill it after the foam subsides.

Salut!

How to open and serve sparkling wine

A thumb in the punt can give added control.

Hold the cork, turn the bottle.

Remove the wire cage.

95

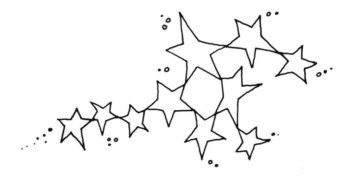

Domaine Chandon
Yountville, California 94599